Have Crutch Will Travel

The Adventures of a Modern Day Calamity Jane

Cale Kenney

Have Crutch Will Travel
Copyright ©2002 by Cale Kenney

For more information, contact:
Cale Kenney
Tell Tale Publishing
P.O. Box 181172
Denver, CO 80218-8823
http://www.howlings.com

Orders:
http://www.howlings.com

First printed edition, limited
ISBN 0-9724-303-0-X

Acknowledgments

A long-awaited first book requires many thanks. I'm grateful first to my 1985 graduate English teacher Gilbert Findlay, a specialist in autobiography at Colorado State University, who encouraged me to write what was difficult, advising, "Some things are so personal you can only tell a stranger."

I want to thank the Edna St. Vincent Millay Colony For The Arts for both the time to collect my thoughts into words, and the space to make a writer-accessible studio out of a studio and an attendant's empty bed. To Ann Ellen Lesser, special thanks for collaborating on universal design for writers.

To Virginia Cornell, who gave me my first job as a sports editor, I owe the thanks of example. I am grateful to Ronni Orlowski and Janet Lurie, Mike Wilson and Jane Hansberry for making Denver a safe place to start over in 1991. A special thanks goes to my sisters, Chrissie, Joanne and Suzy, my bothers, Bill and Steve, and especially to my sister-in-law Liz Kenney who connected me with nurse Charlene Campbell. Charlene stepped out of her comfort range in 1971 and saved the life of a stranger on the road. Thank you. You are the muse from whom I drew the inspiration to begin writing again, in 1993.

To my friend Dorothy Rankin — who edited this book — and to Holly Thompson, thanks for helping make the 'zine, *Howlings: Wild Women of the West*, the success I needed to keep writing short stories for an audience. Thanks also to the wild women writers of Denver who not only contributed their work and voices, but continually made time to write for fun together, especially Ann Vilen, Dana Bennett, Karen Sbrockey, Janie Breggin, Peggy Morris, Susan Bockhoff, Kate Morrell, Shell Noble, Judith Spitzer, Margaret Halsey, Karen Horan, Cynthia Morris, Kathleen Deragon, and Maggie Allen.

To my writer's group, Laura Hershey, Kathy Bougher, Val Phillips, Vicki Rottman, and Dana Zastrow, thanks for your critique and encouragement in early versions, and thanks to Maura Kilcommons, Meg Armstrong, Jim Bernath, John Collier, Kathleen Deragon, Andy Miller, Tommye-K Mayer and Deb Shea — writer's friends to the end.

I want to thank my wonderful literary assistant Andrea Stark who reminded me why I hired her in the first place. To the Denver Women's Art Center and Gallery's Best-of-Show award: One Woman's Words. Your recognition kept me believing in myself even while my writing arms were injured and it seemed all was lost. Thanks is due as well to John and Carol of Colorado V. R. who provided the funds to change platforms from Macintosh to the PC when *Naturally Speaking*™ software was the only way to finish the book. Finally, to Laura Mulvany, who designed the book cover, and Alyson Mulvany, and Barb Scott for helping me get the text into book form.

Most of all, I want to thank Jane Hays, my hero and fellow writer/traveler, author of *Whom The Lord Loveth*. On the drive to Santa Fe to the autobiography workshop, "Writing Yourself," two very different writers found the thirty-years age difference no problem. When I called Jane before the trip — because I might not be able to sit for the long drive — she offered to put a futon in the back seat of her station wagon. I thought she must be heaven-sent. Thanks, Jane, for renewing my faith in God's goodness while I was recovering and giving me support, comfort, and strength on my journey.

Contents

Learning to climb in Eldorado Springs Canyon, Boulder, Colorado, 1986. My progress is measured by the distance from John at the bottom.

Hanging on by fingernails, I learned to stay close to the rock, feel for footholds, look for handholds, and trust my buddy John, who gets smaller each frame.

In this sport, you really have to trust your buddy, touching rock blindly with foot until you are down on the ground. I let go in a free fall backward. Big smile — I've made it one-fourth of the way. You can see John at the bottom, just barely. I am wearing prosthetic sit-socket, "Bertha the Butt," on my left side for balance and protection.

Introduction, The Peer Visit

I must have been showing off the day I met Posie Churchill. I had been invited to visit the Rehab floor of Massachusetts General Hospital (MGH) for a peer visit, which is where an amputee visits others in their hospital beds. My amputation had been performed there at MGH in Boston in 1971. That day in 1975, I was showing three young men who had just lost limbs how a person on one leg can ski. Balancing over my right leg, arms at my side, I stood up straight, facing them, and held my crutches off the ground.

"Imagine the outrigger is like a crutch with a 12-inch ski tip at the end. Okay? Even though it's called three-track skiing, you really don't ride all three ski tips over the snow," I said, explaining that you ski on your one leg and use the outriggers when you needed them to stabilize your balance. "Eventually," I added. "When you get good." I looked pretty good standing there. But I was not good enough to just "ski my ski" back then.

I was interrupted by Muffy Lutzin, a pixie-size woman with dark hair and bright eyes whom I knew as a volunteer from the handicap ski group and who was also the hospital's recreational therapist. "Cale, there's a wonderful woman in the next room who would love to meet you."

Before I went in to meet the woman, I set my crutches against the wall and showed the boys how you turn your ski. I balanced over my one leg, holding the imaginary ski poles. "You keep your knee bent for flexibility." To demonstrate compression, I bent my knee, dropped my hands down to my sides, and turned my knee in either direction, pretending I was skiing. My audience was captivated.

At 24, I practiced yoga and with good balance and a very strong leg, I could swing dance or polka all night — with the right partner — which may be how I developed my strength in the off-season. The year after I graduated from college, I made at least a dozen amputee hospital visits while I looked for a job and continued into my third year of three-track skiing. My own amputation had been done here in Boston at MGH, and I was proud of the young woman survivor I had become.

I had a trick move I called sidestepping, where, for quite a distance, I "walked" laterally, without crutches, using a shimmying toe-first, then-heel maneuver. The day Muffy interrupted me, I was so comfortable in my strength that I left my crutches behind, sidestepped into the other room across the corridor, and met the beaming Posie Churchill.

"I'm so glad to meet you, Ca-el," she said in her thick Boston Brahmin accent.

I side-stepped up to her hospital bed, leaned into it to steady my balance, and extended my hand, for this once without the crutch interference. "Muffy says you've skied all over Europe, Switzerland, and the Alps," I said to the 65-year-old.

Posie spoke in a voice both tremulous and strong, "But I didn't think I would ever ski again after the amputation." Muffy then explained that even at Posie's age, once she was strong enough, she could come up to Sunapee, New Hampshire, and join the ski gang.

"Tell me, how do you do it?" Posie asked, grinning with a toothy, girlish smile.

"It should be easy if you've done it before!" I began. At that point I wished I had some outriggers. Once again I demonstrated the position on my imaginary ski.

"As soon as I heal, I'm going to learn these things called outriggahs," Posie said emphatically, and then she looked over at Muffy, and chuckled deeply as an afterthought. "I suppose, after I learn to use a pros-te-the-sis." Coming to Posie's aid, Muffy and I chimed in on the pronunciation of "pros-thee-sis," and we all laughed about what trouble that word caused most people.

After I'd stood long enough, I excused myself and went back to get my crutches and leave. Hospital visiting could be hard work. But it was part of the ethic of the New England Handicapped Sportsmen (NEHSA) who provided peer visits to hospitals. Many NEHSA members were Vietnam vets who returned from war as amputees and caught the ski bug, quickly becoming full-blown ski bums and instructors. The NEHSA folks had volunteered to teach me several years before, and a lot of hours and several amputee instructors standing around on one leg went into that proposition. It included fitting me for gear, skis and outriggers, and teaching me to control my speed by turning — the hardest thing to do once a neophyte makes it to the top of the hill. NEHSA regularly held race clinics because the elaborate setup of gates as obstacles forced the beginning skier to turn. They would offer the same benefits to Posie.

In a matter of months after meeting the older woman, while I looked for a job and was fit for my first artificial leg, I decided to move from Boston to Colorado. I didn't see Posie again until several years later, when she showed up in my new home town of Winter Park, all smiles in vintage skiwear at the National Handicapped Ski Championships. For years, skiers from across the country gathered there to race and celebrate. In my exciting get-together with old friends from Boston, I heard that the older woman had been quite impressed with me. My amputee friend laughed mockingly as she told me the story.

"Isn't that Cale Kenney something?" Carol reported Posie saying when the new NEHSA brochure with my picture on the cover was distributed.

"What about her?" Carol asked, not about to give me any celebrity status I might have gained by moving away.

"She doesn't even wear an artificial limb!" Posie exclaimed.

"What's so amazing about that?" Carol exclaimed. She had just given up wearing her own hemipelvectomy leg and was getting around more freely now. She may have been a little miffed about the NEHSA bias toward people wearing artificial limbs. Few people had any idea of the special problems of the hemipelvectomy prosthesis, never mind the price. (Most didn't know the difference between us and a hip-disarticulation, who still has both sit-down bones.) However, Posie had an image of me she'd formed from our first meeting, and she was surprised Carol wasn't in awe, too.

"But, she doesn't even use crutches!" Posie said.

Even I laughed at that idea, with the image of myself pogo hopping through my life.

I just love this story — because I'm the hero, of course! But really, because it is so ironic. Wonderfully, it carries the spirit of what those first days of learning to ski were like. The slogan for National Handicap Sports (NHS), the national organization of which NEHSA was a chapter, is: "If I can do this, I can do anything." The way it worked for me was: "If they can do it, I should be able to do it." Yet, there is always a shadow side: the image you learned to project could trap you into an image that betrayed you. Or made others feel you had betrayed them.

Telling my story in those days invited showing off how far I'd come. Yet other times it was appropriate to just show up and visit, and answer questions before and after surgery, especially for someone with cancer — or osteomylitis or another disease — who had time to think before amputation. In these cases, I'd tell a more modest story of wholeness and survival. But each visit became a healing when we shared our stories. I vividly remember one visit where I was called in — not for the patient but for the staff.

The patient, a lovely young girl from the town next to mine, had been taken on a harrowing ride by the drunk driver of a motorcycle, who caused them to be broadsided by a car. Her injuries did not involve amputation from gangrene like mine; her pelvis was split open and now held together by a Hoffman device, a steel contraption with pins that went through flesh, so the bones could knit back together. She still had her parts but was in excruciating pain.

I was called in because "she cries all the time." A psychology supervisor invited me to speak to the unit nurses who had become so demoralized by her suffering that they allegedly became callous to her cries for help. The psychologist lectured on the language of crying. Some cries both express pain and relieve it, she explained. Grief had a different sound to it, and yet another pitch signaled a call for help. The nurses were asked to "listen," translate, and respond accordingly.

Realizing my long period of misery was now the past — except for phantom reminders — I called up the memories of my hospitalization and shared with the staff how I'd cried with as many messages. When I spoke of the pain, I was awed and humbled by my role as a witness to the nurses.

When I went in to meet Patty, she asked, "Were you once really like me?" I nodded, speechless. Seeing her lying in her bed, three months longer than my stay, the flesh wounds seeping, I concluded that my losses shortened my time of suffering. I felt lucky when I first went to meet her.

I admired the way she came right out with it, but it didn't make it easy to answer her when she asked. "Did it feel like you fell on to the bar of a boy's bicycle?" I nodded, and I didn't feel lucky anymore, because right there I broke through something. I couldn't put it into words yet, but I felt like a hole had been blown right through the middle of me. It was the only peer visit where I left with a dark foreboding. I sensed more grief ahead.

[Later, I learned as I aged that the human skeleton must compensate for the loss of the pelvis; usually by developing a scoliosis, and in my case chronic back pain, but in 1999, I paid with injuries to my arms, simply because without the second sit-down bone, you have to hold your body upright with help from your arms and hands. Thus, the upper extremities are more susceptible to "overuse" injuries.] I was protected from the knowledge of these future realities by my youthful arrogance and denial for at least ten years.

Many years later, when I no longer had time or energy for these hospital visits, my stories became "written visits." I stopped doing hospital visits in the '90s. Thereafter, when therapists who saw me as the epitome of rehabilitation asked me to visit one of their patients, I sent one of my adventure stories.

I may never have written the stories that form Part II of this book, "The Adventures," had I not been knocked on the side of the head by a synchronistic event. After a reconstructive surgery in 1987, I was left with a higher level of nerve pain. It got so bad I wondered why I'd been spared in 1971. My quality of life suffered greatly. In 1992, I met the first of my many angels, Charlene Campbell, the woman who'd saved my life on the road 20 years before. Charlene is the "voice" in chapter two that reached into the darkness and told me I was alive, and not in hell as I feared.

I view this book as an intimate witness in "Part I, The Impact." I'm back to showing off in "Part II, The Adventures." I hope amputees can relate to both.

Meeting Charlene inspired me to change my code of silence about my accident. As a journalist writing a first-person piece, crutches, frankly, were a distraction. Every crutch begs to tell a story, and I didn't want to distract the reader. I always assumed the viewpoint of a bi-ped. However, after meeting Charlene I asked, "Why not write down all those stories about the calamities I've had on crutches that have made my friends laugh?" So for the last ten years, besides teaching and freelance publishing, I've been a storyteller about "the glory days" and my misadventures as a one-legged enthusiast of the outdoors.

As I write today it is from my "bedmobile," with voice recognition software for typing and crutches for short distance walking. But as soon as I get a sit-down prosthesis that works, I'll begin a new series of travels from a power wheel chair.

The last story is called "Calamity Jane," my nickname in middle school, whose mention provoked shame because the calamitous stories that earned the moniker covered up the truth of a troubled home and my anguished, bumbling efforts to get to my new middle school on time. It wasn't until I was an adult and read the real Calamity Jane's autobiography that I realized being compared to this female pioneer was a compliment. Born 100 years apart — she in 1852 and I in 1952, — we both went west. We both pushed the limits of our gender and person. I could identify with her love of adventure and the outdoors, and with her strong desire to venture beyond the conventional into a new frontier. And just as strong, her desire to write about it.

Finally, I included pictures because I think it's fun to find pictures in books about real people. I called Posie Churchill the other day. She's 91, and though she didn't remember my name, she told me she wished she did. I asked her if she remembered skiing with me. "No, but I wish I were skiing now," she said, not missing a beat. Then she added, "Your voice has invigorated me. Do you think we could call each other and get reacquainted?" That's Posie.

I love the people I've met on this path of accidental adventure: NSCD, ACA, NHS, caregivers everywhere. This book is dedicated to them and to my old friend Fred Tassone, who knew how to have fun and liked to say, "Nobody said it was going to be easy." And he proceeded to make it look that way.

The Impact

May 1971, Lory State Park, Northampton, Massachusetts. Preparing for a
cartwheel, I'm wearing the "$27 bathing suit."

Miss American Pie

(1996 Written for Tattered Cover reading)

In 1968, at 16, I was a "fox." With my all-American-girl looks and bedroom-blue eyes I wanted to be the Marilyn Monroe of my neighborhood, or maybe Goldie Hawn — with a bosom. Or perhaps Miss America, only short. I could picture myself walking the dais in my high heels, turning my derrière to just the right angle, smiling and waving. I'd be making up for all those years when — as a freckled, skinny, ugly duckling — I squinted into the sun as the camera invited me in for what I'd feel later was a false reading.

Until I was 15, something wasn't right. From grade six to grade eight I'd cringe at my school pictures. My dishwater blonde hair didn't fall like rain from my crown like mod London model Jean Shrimpton's golden bangs; it squiggled over my forehead like worms, stopping short of hiding scraggly eyebrows. Since I would never take my glasses off for a picture, I had to squinch my eyes to see straight, and smiled a crooked smile.

I'd look at those school pictures and object. *I was meant to be a beauty.* I could feel this destiny in my bones as they stretched from four-feet-nine-inches at age 10 to five-foot-one at 15. Since my own mother — who had borne eight children in ten years — had no figure to speak of, this destiny must have been foretold by photos of her when she was young.

They called her "Brick," as in built like a brick outhouse. She had legs up to here and face and hair like Hepburn — Katharine, that is. She posed in those '30s short shorts, and the photographer caught her curves — from cheekbones to chin, from breasts to hips, to shapely calves and well-turned ankles. *I would be like her.*

In the '60s, short-shorts were not popular. Bermuda shorts were the trend. Indian madras, from which the shorts were made, not only disguised the thigh but discouraged showing any shape. Even if you got them wet enough to reveal the thigh, the madras would bleed an awful mess of colors down your legs. Not that I ever got wet anyway when I was a teen. I never went into the pool at a party, never mind the ocean, for fear of the kinky effect the water might have on my straight-haired look, into which I had literally ironed my naturally curly hair.

Peering down at those pictures of my mother in her old albums, I'd think: If I could get my hands on a pair of those short shorts, I'd wear them! I experimented with blue jeans, pulling the woof from the warp until I had denim fringes hanging from two inches below my crotch to my upper thigh, like Daisy Mae in the Li'l Abner cartoons. When granny dresses came into vogue in the early '70s, I protested with mini-mini skirts. I had legs and, go Betty Grable, I was gonna show 'em.

Who knew where this exhibitionism came from. I knew by 16 if I could control my unruly hair, and make it a shade or two blonder, I would fit so snugly into a playboy bunny outfit that you'd have to pull the staple out of <u>her</u> belly button to separate me from the fantasy girl. I would have power like I never did when I was 10, when I caught my Dad staring at 16-year old Nanette down the street. Once invisible like me, Nanette had recently grown into her pulchritudinous young maidenhood. She oozed some power that made my father gawk.

I learned pulchritudinous for a spelling bee that I won in the ninth grade.

As a playboy bunny I would have that same power over men, but I would use it discreetly and mainly for the betterment of society, like Mata Hari did. I devoured the playboy bunny bios for some sense of politics and found none. I didn't see how they could influence history without some kind of political platform. I mean, what was it all about? There had to be some point to winning a beauty competition!

I feared women were the moral power behind men. Wasn't the influence of their beauty the way in which power was transferred? How would they know how to influence the guy to vote if they didn't have a wide scope of information about Vietnam, or global issues, or if they didn't have their own moral values and passions?

At 14, when nature hadn't yet taken her course, using the age-old art of glamour, I induced in myself a likeness to Cheryl Tiegs, a model whose picture I carried in my wallet as though it were a picture of myself walking out of a plane waving to the camera. I began with ironing my hair, first the bangs. I plucked my eyebrows and lengthened my lashes with Baby Oil. Instead of pancake makeup, I kept a California model's color all year using Instant Tanning Lotion by Coppertone — except for the time I used too much and streaked my face orange. That at least made my teeth look whiter.

Around 15, I started getting noticed. The motorheads down the street cat-called from their garage assessing my build — "Hey, small chassis, wide ovals." I knew that metaphor was a compliment. It seemed I grew into that valued status overnight: One day I was transparent, the next I couldn't cross the street without some truck driver whistling at me. It was several years before the attention got old. When you've been starved for attention, for affection, you take it wherever you can get it. When you've had enough, you move on to something new.

At 18 something new awaited. At college I basked in the glow of ideas and knowledge. As a sociology student at UMass Amherst, I loved my studies. I appreciated male attention, when polite, but I hated the meat markets of the barrooms and fraternities, where women were invited in to commingle, like sheep led to slaughter. I liked being appreciated for my mind, my wit, my political passions, my ideas, and the way I looked; at 18 this was new for me. This was how I was attracted to my friend Mark, through this combination.

But then came that fateful day in May 1971. For several years afterward, I craved that kind of obnoxious male attention I had learned to despise. I longed to be ogled, whistled at, lusted after like a sex kitten. I longed to be a lamb led to slaughter, lavished with any kind of notice other than sympathy, pity or mere curiosity.

Those days passed, too, though with certain reservations. By 20, I began to love myself again. I learned to make the best of what I had. But at times, I have stood in the shadow of that other girl's might-have-been.

Facing the mirror as an older woman, feeling the loss of power that comes with age and diluted beauty, in my 40s I'm taking honest stock of my girlhood dreams, and struggle to know what matters now.

I ask myself, what did I miss during those years of male attention that feed a young woman's self-esteem? After age 19, I designed and sewed my own clothing, hiding my body from the waist down with empire dresses and jumpers that went to my ankle.

Though I lost the option to run, jump, and tumble as a cheerleader, a role to which I had aspired for years in high school, I did find a sport in which I could express myself. As a competitive skier I won ground on more than one lost front.

To what extent did my accident restrict my options for love and marriage? I never got the man of my dreams after my dreams were shattered; I had boyfriends, but I never married. With arms reserved for crutches, romantic fantasies of walking the beach hand-in-hand remained just that — fantasies. With a body violated by radical surgery, I lost the chance to have children, while never properly losing my virginity. I am only now consciously grieving the woman I never was.

When a friend who knew me when we were 16 remarked, "I never could have survived what you went through," I surprised myself, telling her: "I didn't. That girl had to die, and someone new grew in her place." In 1972 a popular song alluded to the music dying, and I made an immediate connection that the all-American girl who sang along with the songs on the car radio, made out in the back of a Chevy, and whose wish it was to be the object of every boy's dreams, would not be in my destiny.

For most of us there comes a day when our innocence dies, and we are forced to say goodbye to a kinder world. May 24, 1971 — at 19 — was the day I died.

Top: 1960, Bellingham Avenue, Revere. First row sitting: Kathleen, Billy, and baby Steven . Standing next to Calamity Cale, Chrissie. Bottom: Cale (l) on phone in front with Billy; Cousin Elizabeth Corsaro, Chrissie Kenney, and Cousin Steve Corsaro.

Spring 1971, Mark Robinson. Mark's mother, Dottie, gave me this photo of him in skydiving gear taken not long before the accident. When I took the photo out of its frame, 30 years later, it disintegrated.

The Voice

I was making a bathing suit the day Mark Robinson asked me to go for a ride on his new motorcycle. He showed up at the second floor lounge of Melville House. "CaleCaleCale," he said bursting through the doors.

When I looked up to see his green eyes, I smiled back. I don't remember why, but he had recently started greeting me by saying my name three times fast. Leaning over the table surface I had converted into a cutting board, I snipped off the last piece of interfacing.

"MarkMarkMark, I'm making a bathing suit!" I announced. He stood leaning against the doorjamb, in cutoff jeans and a t-shirt, his arms crossed in a relaxed pose; but the excitement in his voice told me something unusual was up.

"So, this is where you are! I tried to call you. Are you ready for a ride?"

"Yes!" Then it came to me. "You got the bike working! Sure! Soon as I put this stuff away." I must admit that, considering how long I had been looking forward to this maiden voyage, I almost didn't want to go. I was nearly finished with the bathing suit and wanted to see what it looked like on me. But I had been longing for a ride ever since I heard he was getting a bike, and this was my last free day. Tomorrow was my French final, and then my freshman year at the University of Mass at Amherst was over. "It'll take me two minutes," I added.

11

"Okay!" he said, halfway out the door, "I'll bring the bike around and meet you at my dorm then." He bounded down the stairs in that way of his, on the balls of his feet, like an Indian in magic moccasins. Part Cherokee, Mark was about five-foot nine or ten, lean and all muscle. I had only recently learned that he was a track star in high school. He was forever surprising me; he wore his hair long, like Prince Valiant, and he told me he had an alter ego named Christopher Robin. I missed the literary allusion because I'd never read Winnie the Pooh when I was young. Instead I imagined a bird named Christopher. Mark was smart, taking courses in a pre-med track, and he didn't seem like the kind of boy who would ride a motorcycle. But then, I'd never known anyone who parachuted from airplanes, either. Mark had just finished taking his first skydive.

We met my first semester, his third, in an 8 a.m. French class. He would come over evenings to Herman Melville House, my all-girl dormitory where I was also working evenings as a lobby security guard. We coached each other in French and talked about our other classes. I'd been introduced to Aristotle, Socrates and Plato in my Classics 101 course and to the Greek tragedy writers, Sophocles and Euripides, in English class. Because he was a sophomore, Mark had taken many of the courses the year before, and he talked about them as eagerly as I did.

"What did you think of Plato's "Analogy of the Caves?" he asked me one night, a frown darkening his face. "Did you get that at all?"

"Oh, yeah! Didn't you? But I like the tragedies more." He was nodding his head, so I asked, "What do you think of Oedipus Rex? Wasn't that the most amazing story? The way he learned his future in advance — that he would kill his mother and father — so he leaves home just so he won't do those things, and..." Mark interrupted me.

"He ends up meeting his real father on the road, kills him, and the kingdom gives him his own mother as a reward. I know. That was great." Then, "Yeah, no matter what, the Greeks think your fate is decided before you are born," he said.

"But the existentialists believe you create your own destiny. Free will and all that," I countered.

"What do you think?" he asked me.

"I believe you can be whoever you want to be." Then I hastily added a qualifier; I was taking a course in existential literature: "Of course, your life is somewhat determined by your social class and, to a certain extent, your upbringing."

"And your genes," he said.

"Yeah — but I still believe we create our own existence." I ended my definitive statement on Life with an opening to him: "Do you think your fate was decided before you were born?"

He was a serious conversationalist, and as he stopped to think, his face took on a different cast. "I don't know, actually. Didn't Oedipus have free will?" His strong, square jaw and high cheekbones became more prominent in this mood. "He's the one who decided not to stay with his family."

"Yeah, but in trying to avoid his fate, he walked right into it," I said.

"So, who decided his fate, then?" He gave me an opening, so I prattled on.

"It was the Oracle at Delphi. No. Was it the gods who decided his fate, and the oracle just told him? And he thought that, knowing it, he could escape it."

"Yeah. But that was the very thing that caused his fate," then he asked me the question that made me think. "So, did he have free will?"

"I see what you mean," I said, liking him more for the challenge of conversation he always presented and which I had never experienced in high school.

Other times, Mark and I had debates over ethics and which laws were more important, those of the individual or those of society. He sometimes took the side of society because I was very much an advocate of the individual, but we both flip-flopped from time to time.

In a contemplative literature class, I learned that a Jewish theologian, Martin Buber, believed that God exists in the intersections where we humans experience true dialogue — in the honest give and take of relationship, the purpose of which is to understand and accept though not necessarily agree. Mark and I were both under 20, and our conversations really were often just debates on an intellectual level, but I thought of them as spiritual because we both believed in a Divinity.

Second semester I worked lobby security in another dorm, a 20-story high-rise building in the same part of campus where Mark and I lived, known as Southwest. Though UMass was a land-grant, agriculture-based institution, this side of campus was a city in miniature —

five high-rise dormitories and a half-dozen or so three-story lowrises on a section of campus paved with cement and accented with more glass than grass. At the beginning of that second semester, Mark would stop by to visit with me and end up walking me home. I was sure I was just the last on a long list of people he checked in on in the evenings; he was a sociable and popular person.

When we walked across the square, I'd saunter slowly, tired from work, and he would dance around me to slow himself down. Often we'd pause outside his dorm and sit on the hot-air vents, having discussions that evolved from intellectual to more personal.

"When school is over I'm going to Lake Placid — in the Adirondacks, you know? — to get a job as a waitress for the summer," I told him as we both leaned our backs against the brick building.

"That's in upstate New York?" he asked. "Why there?" He stretched his legs out in front of him, so I did too.

"Oh, I used to live in Saranac Lake when I was 16, and I still have friends there. I'm applying at the Whiteface Inn." I told him how I wanted to learn to water ski. I planned to reunite with my good friend Patty and to have plenty of beer parties down by Lake Ampersand where her fiancé's family lived.

"Waitressing, huh? Have you ever done that work before?"

"No. Are you kidding? I've only had one other real job besides babysitting and cleaning people's houses. One year I ironed for $1/hour. But how hard can it be to take orders and pick up plates?"

"I don't know." He shrugged and looked over at me. "What was your real job?"

"I was a money-checker girl at Skill Right."

He narrowed his eyes. "What's a Skill Right?"

"Don't laugh, okay? It's a bingo joint on Revere Beach." I described how the gaming establishment where I'd worked made bingo legal.

"What a trip! So you did this in high school?" He smiled at me after my long dissertation on Skill Right. His smile was warm and blinding; it filled his whole face with an uncommon openness.

"Yep. It was my first job where they took out taxes. It paid for my clothes and movies, and every Wednesday night on payday, we went to the China Roma and had Chinese food."

"I always thought Revere Beach was a strange place," he teased, "but an Italian Chinese Restaurant?" He looked to make sure I didn't have an elbow coming his way.

"I always thought it would be pretty bad to be from Danvers, myself!" I countered.

Mark was from a town about 40 miles north of me up the coast, called Danvers. The state mental hospital there made "going to Danvers" a joke when I was a Revere street kid. It actually was a nice suburban town; it had beautiful beaches, not tacky like Revere, the place where I grew up as a kid. A city of 40,000 in the 1960's, Revere was home to the first public beach in the United States. But over the past several decades, the city had been corrupted by Mafia influences. Urban renewal in Revere took the form of

16

mysterious fires, supposedly set so insurance money could be collected.

"Did Skill Right pay okay?" he asked.

"Not as much as waitressing. Trust me," I laughed.

We were both quiet then.

"So, you're going to New York before you even know if you've got a job." He laughed at me again and then spoke, not shyly. "I was going to ask if you wanted to come with me sometime this summer to Plum Island." He had wanted me to meet his sister Wendy who lived in another dorm in Southwest, but beyond that, which I assumed would happen before semester's end, I hadn't considered how we might stay in touch. I also hadn't realized this might be our last day together until next year.

I was silent. Plum Island. I'd heard about this nature preserve on the Atlantic coast, but the one time I'd set out with girlfriends to see it, we drove past it and ended up on the coast of New Hampshire instead.

"How would we get there?" I asked. "Hitchhike?"

"On my motorcycle. I told you I'm getting a bike, didn't I?"

"A motorcycle?" I raised my voice a couple of octaves with excitement. "I love motorcycles! I'm going to buy a small red Honda motorbike this summer." I then chattered on about the romance of the road and my attraction to motorcycles. I told him how, at the amusement park on Revere Beach, I had developed a strong fascination with Harleys and the men and women who rode them. The rough-looking men scared me, but I didn't tell Mark that. He told me he didn't have a Harley, but a small BSA road bike he'd been fixing up so he could get it running before the end of the semester. That conversation was in March.

By the end of April, each of us had our troubling experiences. Sharing the stories with each other was an unexpected solace. I had just lost a friend to suicide and had to break the news to his parents, who were on campus when it happened. Mark was feeling pressure from friends to return feelings for a woman who loved him. He was obviously not ready. He told me his friends thought he should see a psychiatrist, and I could tell this had unsettled him. I believe he felt safe with me because I, too, was a person who shied away from intimacy.

Before leaving for his dormitory, I couldn't resist trying on the unfinished bathing suit. I was already wearing my favorite — and only — bathing suit, from which I had made a pattern for this one. My old suit was red, white and blue with circles and wavy lines and rode low on my hips and under my belly. I loved the way it fit, but it had begun to fade. The reason I couldn't part with it was sentimental. The day we bought it was the first time my mother had taken me shopping for such an intimate item. On that day she not only acknowledged that I was becoming a young woman but seemed to honor it.

I remember the top was simple, but cut low enough to be very sexy. In the dressing room that day when I shopped with my mother, I liked it so much, I was sure she'd veto it. When she asked if I was ready, I came out from behind the drapery and looked down in embarrassment.

"Oh, how lovely," my mother said softly. She was probably surprised to see me in so little clothing; I was extremely modest at home. "And it fits you perfectly. How much is it, dear?" That was the next hurdle. I had no idea how much she was willing to spend. She seemed to deliberate, and then the saleslady came over to tell us it was on sale from $40 to $27.

"Oh, we have to get it now! Do you like it, dear?" This one day of bonding helped heal the hurt of several years of unintended neglect, when my mother was absent from home. For at least three years she worked and then went to the hospital to be with my younger sister Kathleen, who was dying of leukemia. This bathing suit transaction was a rite of passage, a nod to go ahead and be a woman without shame, with the young woman's body I was growing into, despite my father's violation of my innocence.

Back in my dorm room, I took off my old bathing suit top and put on the unfinished one. Admiring my tan lines, I congratulated myself on a perfect fit. I rode my hands over my hips and held the bottom against the old bathing suit to see how it matched. It looked good, much better than the first version I had made several days earlier. I decided I would give that one to my younger sister Chrissie, who was a size or more larger than my petite self.

Standing on my tiptoes, I pirouetted before the mirror for one last look at the top. I then threw all my sewing gear into a box, shoved it under the bed, and ran into the lounge to return the sewing machine to its place, downstairs in a closet. I was finally ready, and I nearly tripped as I ran out of the dorm to get to Mark's place.

When I got to his door, Mark took one look at me and turned around to dig something out of a box. He handed me a helmet and looked excited but serious.

"You're going to need a helmet. I've got a jacket you can borrow, too." These were both disappointing to hear.

"But what about the wind in my hair and the grasshoppers in my teeth?" I was wearing cutoff shorts, sandals and a tank top. I was going for the full spring effect, and I was serious.

Mark laughed, taking the options out of my protest. "If we had time, I'd make you go back and wear a pair of long pants." I could tell then he disapproved of my sandals. I had no idea I would have to wear so much special gear. He handed me a jean jacket, and we headed for the parking lot. I asked him if we could drop off a roll of film I'd taken of our whole gang at the State Park in Northampton the week before. I couldn't have known then how precious those pictures would become. With the film bulging in my back pocket, I settled into the back of the bike. We headed in the direction of downtown, and I ran into the drug store before we headed out for the open road.

Springtime comes full of promise to Amherst: birds chirping, grass shining out of rolling green pastures, and the perfume of lilacs and apple blossoms wafting in the air. We reveled in it. On the way to Sunderland and points northwest, the Berkshires beckoned. After a semester of hard work I was ready for springtime's promise of summer. In a few days, I would be at Saranac Lake.

I was glad not to be going back to my hometown of Revere. I wanted to leave my family and that past behind. There would be relatives and good friends to stay with in Saranac while I found my summer job.

But I was not thinking of the summer while riding with Mark. The rush of air and scenery were breathtaking and intoxicating. Surrounded by the muffled roar of the BSA bike, I was thinking, "Finally, we're getting out of town. Finally I'm riding a motorcycle."

I gave a squeal of delight and yelled to Mark, "I'm so glad you came to get me!"

When a pickup truck pulled next to us, I yelled to the driver, "Hey, Easy Rider!"

"What?" Mark yelled back at me. Even at a standstill, verbal communication on the motorcycle was difficult, so I didn't bother to repeat myself and just hugged him. He then looked back at me through his rear view mirror, and I remember his green eyes, how they sought mine, how he flashed his smile at me, how it felt to be so close to him. At the green light we vroomed away from the pickup and turned onto Route 116, the stretch of road that led to Sunderland and beyond to the Berkshire Hills.

Leaving the urban quadrant of the University and the quaint town of Amherst, I was surprised to see the agricultural campus surroundings so quickly. "Ooh, Look! Cows!" I poked Mark again; this time he smiled back and nodded. I relaxed back into the seat and hung on for the ride. Finally, away from it all — the dorms, the work, the study, the status of pedestrian. It was past 3:30, and we wouldn't be out for long, but just this much was wonderful.

Coming around a bend on Route 116 near Plum Tree Road, I never saw, and I don't think Mark did either, the car that veered straight out of its lane and into ours. Life can be gone in a minute, in a second, and it was this quickly that we were hit head-on at 55 miles an hour by someone I later learned was an uninsured motorist. He was driving his girlfriend's car and not paying attention to the road as he bent down to pick up some papers that had fallen off the seat. At the curve in the road we all met our destinies.

I was told Mark's leg was ripped from his body, and he died instantly of a broken neck. I was thrown 20 feet through the air and hit a utility pole with my pelvis, crushing it and fracturing both legs. I then landed on the ground, lacerating my left elbow and hand. I didn't know at the instant of impact what had happened. It didn't even register that I had been on a bike in the countryside. The force of the impact sent my body immediately into shock and all I could figure was that I had been hit from behind by a bus and then run over.

There on the ground near Plum Tree Road, I lay trying to get up, commanding my arms to push me off the ground and stand up. Trying to push my voice out of my chest, emitting sounds that felt far away, I wondered if I still had my teeth. I expected to hear myself groan and raise my hand to my mouth, but I couldn't follow through on the intention. I realized I had no control over my body.

"Please help me get up," I cried, sensing people around me.

I heard a murky hubbub, a mumbling, and felt a sensation much like lying in a gutter of brackish water, the texture of ugliness and despair.

Finally, I made out one distinct sound. It was a woman's voice, clear like a mountain stream trickling over rocks saying, "You're going to be all right. You have been in a motorcycle accident; the ambulance is on the way. We are here with you. Just hang in there."

"Where's Mark?" I knew enough to know that I had been with Mark Robinson, even though I didn't make the connection that we'd been hit on a motorcycle.

"We're taking care of him. Don't you worry."

I fell back into the infernal blackness of shock and trauma, and I wondered where I was. Could this be hell?

This is hell, I thought, as I tumbled and bumped into dark corners of space with what was left of my conscious mind.

After trying for an eternity to push against the ground to get up, I clung to the earth like a barnacle. I held onto the firmament beneath my chest while the world spun round and round like a disk, trying to fling me off into the void.

The blackness was so thick and deep and buffeting; it felt like a tornado. I hallucinated — watching Ferris wheels spinning madly out of control and monkeys and human children, bellies swelled with malnutrition, swirling through space screaming. I held on with my consciousness, my mind begging: "Please let this be a dream." The nightmare raged while I clung to whatever reality said, "This is not hell," and whatever shred of light could make me believe, "This may be a dream."

My mind was like a commander reining his soldiers in after sending them out to die, bringing me back to the feminine Voice that responded whenever I could speak.

"Where's Mark?" I cried again.

"He is here. The ambulance is on the way," and I was flung off again, flying raggedly through space, my body along for a ride to a destination that did not require a body. When the chaos chose direction, I felt my whole being sucked out of my body into a skinny, black vortex of particles, dust, then colors, purple and green, and then a brighter light, which felt as though it could have been a release, but it didn't feel right. It didn't feel natural. I didn't want to go. I was fighting it, trying to wake up. Wake up, open your eyes and wake up, I told myself. I would find myself conscious again, but I couldn't see, and barely could hear through the rushing of what might have been death's wings. I called out again for Mark.

"He is here," the words were deliberate, carefully spoken. "We are taking care of him. Don't you worry," I heard and was hurled again, flung through space, feeling annihilation a moment away. The only hope my conscious mind could hold was that I wasn't really in hell but having a dream of it. A dream will end. I will wake up. It is only a nightmare.

It took the ambulance 20 minutes to get there.

Urgent voices, staccato interrogations reaching into the roiling darkness. "What is your name? Can you tell us where you live? What is your mother's phone number?"

I was a smart aleck in high school, the best wit in grade seven, class clown in grade eight. Reflexively, I wanted to joke: "I can only give you my name, rank and serial number." But my mind suspected what my body already knew: This was not time to joke. "Bernice Kenney, 168 Beach Street, 284-5412. In Revere." I gave them the words, and I fell again into hell. Hell was dark, cold, and like a tornado, never still.

I heard them saying, "Get that bathing suit off her," and I tried to oppose them, crying, "Don't ruin my $27 bathing suit!" Now struggling out of a swamp of darkness, I couldn't see, but I could hear. But no one seemed to listen to me. Until my mother came.

I heard my aunts' voices first, their tonalities the same as my mother's, and then I could hear the resonance of my mother's voice. What relief! Ma! It was like I was hooked into her from the other end of a tube that threatened to suck the life out of me. She kept pulling me back in with her voice.

I heard my sister Chris say my name. "Chrissie," I remember saying. "I made you a bathing suit." I then imagined us both on the beach. We were children, but we were both wearing the red bathing suit.

"Where am I?" I asked my mother.

"You're in the hospital, dear. In Northampton." My mother's voice sounded grave and sad.

"In Northampton? Where's Mark?"

She didn't answer.

"He's dead, isn't he, Ma?" I didn't believe it was possible when I thought to ask, but as soon as the words were out, I knew it was probable.

"Yes, dear," she said in a voice that leaned over and cradled me. "He didn't make it. Mark didn't make it." She said this as though she had known him, too. Mark's mother called my mother the next day, and from then on it was as if my mother had known Mark, too.

Mark didn't make it. Some piece of me died. It was hard to imagine Mark being gone. So I didn't for a while. It went eventually to a little place in my heart's memory that I now keep sacred. This place is translucent silver, soft pink inside, like a bowl, and filled with tears that have turned to pearls, and I keep images, mostly, but with some people I keep conversations and shapes of shells, feathers and stuff that makes me cry so my heart can wring out my memory cells, all of them. The smell of Paula's hair; Mark's smile; Phil's wild, reddish curls; Mark Newman's rippling laughter; Aunt Mary's sing-song phone announcements — "Carolyn Sue, it's for you;" Dad's morning smell with bacon and eggs all hours of the day; the soft skin on Ma's face and her voice that I sometimes hear at night when I'm done remembering. And in my body, I feel the pain of their having been here and gone, and how that surely hurt. I just know it did. I don't care what anyone says; you don't go quietly, gently. It's a terrible ripping from the earth.

None of those I know, who died, wanted to go. You only want to go when it hurts so much you would have to die to feel better. I know that one, too.

I couldn't see the outlines of the hospital room, but the people, their voices and their faces all felt like some Salvador Dali mural, surrealistically floating above me. I tried to piece together the puzzle. How could my two aunts from New York be in the same place as Dick Fowler from the counseling center at Southwest. And how could my mother and my sister travel to Northampton? My mother didn't know how to drive; my sister didn't have a license. If my brother Billy had driven them, why hadn't he spoken to me yet?

26

My sister told me later that they had not been able to reach my father, who didn't have a phone but did have a car. She said she convinced my mother to hitchhike along the Massachusetts Turnpike. This was in the early '70s when hitchhiking was not normally done by non-hippie adults. They got to Northampton two hours after they got the phone call informing them I was hurt and might not make it.

"When we got there, they had your body up in this huge sling and your leg was sticking out high above your head. They said that as fast as they were pouring blood into you, you were losing it out your pelvis. Ma said the halls were lined with college kids who showed up every day for three days to give you blood."

My sister Chris is shy to mention this in front of other people, but she told me that when she saw me, and I was talking about a bathing suit — which sounded so strange and trivial to her, and probably foreign as hell because as long as we lived in the same house, I never let her touch a stitch of my hand-sewn outfits — when she saw me like that in the sling, she felt a whoosh of energy transferred to my spirit from hers, leaving her weak and drained. Many people said they prayed for me, even those who did not normally pray. Perhaps I received their energy infusions each of the times I emerged to consciousness again in the next three weeks. I only know that my consciousness went in and out, and often it was voices and the words that pulled me back again, though sometimes it was a face.

"Cale, we are going to amputate your leg." I heard that one.

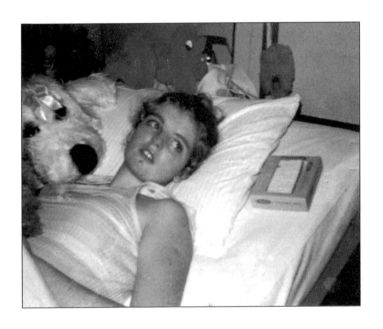

1971, I didn't like having my picture taken because my hair was falling out.

Under the Big Tent
(Chapter 5, Miss American Pie)

While my body lay hanging in a pelvic sling with newly donated blood pouring in and out of me, they battled for my life at Cooley-Dickinson Hospital until they realized they were losing. When they could not contain the spread of gangrene from my leg to my hip, Dr. Hinckley called a surgeon who had great talent in amputating to contain cancer cells that had spread to women's hips and pelvises.

His name was Dr. Hedberg. He was like a god to me. When the Cooley-Dickenson doctors could do no more for me, my mother told me, "There is a doctor at Mass General in Boston who can help us. Dr. Hedberg." After I knew about Mark's death, it became real to me that I could die too. I then repeated the doctor's name; it became a mantra to me in my desperate effort to survive.

"Doctor Hedberg" were the last words on my mother's lips as they loaded me into the ambulance for the risky transfer.

I don't know all the names for the physical states of shock and breakdown I was in, but I do know the 90-minute trip only took an hour speeding down the Mass Pike while I was in a state of siege.

In the ambulance, my lungs, kidneys and liver collapsed, and by the time I reached the emergency room, I heard voices talking urgently, "You better get that thing in her right now or she's going to go on us."

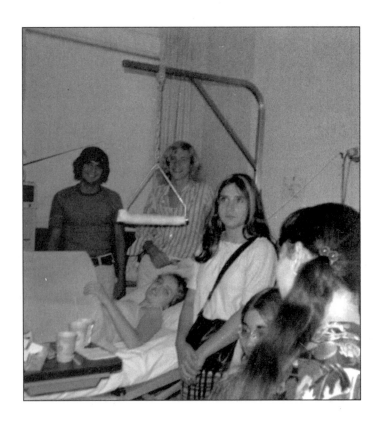

1971, Under the Big Tent. My mother was always taking pictures. In this one I pose with high school friends; clockwise, Desi, Eddie, my best friend Gale, Berta and Paula.

Although I felt like I soared off the stretcher, I'm sure I couldn't have moved more than a twitch. But I declared, "I am not going to die! Where's Dr. Hedberg?!" My hope in Hedberg was one of two elements of my survival.

Many times, I heard what was being said between doctors and nurses over my body. Rarely was I able also to see them, but the one image I remember was like something one would see through a fish-eye lens. The ambulance arrived at the emergency room with sirens blaring, and into my distorted field of perception peered these doctor/nurse faces of incompetence. "You're all a bunch of spics! Where's Dr. Hedberg?" I screamed. I felt like I must meet him right then or I couldn't hold on. And I called out for my mother. She was the other element.

My mother told me about my arrival at MGH in the ambulance from her perspective.

"You had a very high temperature, you were in shock, and they weren't taking you at the emergency ward right away. They had me wait. Then Doctor Hedberg came. [I told him] I wanted to see the surgery.

"You were yelling you wouldn't let them do anything to you unless I came in. So Dr. Hedberg let me. I came in after the [second] above-the-knee amputation and held the stump while he hit it with an instrument, and he said, 'There's healthy tissue.' And I was so happy, I said 'Hallelujah!'

"Everything happened so fast. They thought they had caught the gangrene. But then they had to do another amputation, this time of your hip and the [floater] rib," my mother told me. That means they watched it for three days to see if they had caught the gangrene. I wonder why they didn't catch it sooner, although these are the thoughts you have to censor.

I interviewed my mother the year before she died and am lucky to have her taped testimony, but she wasn't sure about the sequence of events. Looking for some progression of the amputations, I turned to the notes I had copied from Mass General Hospital's medical library. Though it was 10 years after the amputation, the notes had immediacy and a vitality I would not have expected. The very syntax of the doctor's notes conveyed to me the emotion — or sometimes a seeming lack of it — these menders of people felt toward their subjects.

I read that when I arrived at Mass General I was taken to surgery shortly after my emergency room admission. My ER notes read: "*Severe pelvic fracture and severe laceration of the perineum.*"

The comment is made in the ER notes on the same date that, "her labia are cold, swollen, and blue." That's a sign they were dead. I was absolutely chilled reading this, not wanting to think about any of the further death to my most private parts, yet knowing I would experience much more if I were to follow this paper trail through the next month of trauma at MGH. I didn't consider that reading this material might cause further trauma; I was intent on uncovering the truth about my unconscious past.

On May 27, 1971, the doctor's notes reveal they removed the pelvic packs. Two days later, "*She is a little agitated, keeps asking whether she is to be operated on tonight."* This is the evening of the day they informed me they were going to amputate further.

According to the next notes, on May 30, Dr. Hedberg performed a hip disarticulation; the description of the operation is fascinating but grim enough for me to turn the page and not look at it again.

On June 2 and 3, the nurse's notes report, they performed débridement (pronounced de-breed-ment), but the gangrene they had tried to prevent from spreading to nearby flesh had outfoxed their antibiotics. Doctor Hedberg's sketchy notes report briefly on the next few days, but I find that in their sequence, these are enough to raise anxiety in me, as though this report were made today. It occurs to me that I never saw him when he had a look of concern. My visual memories of Dr. Hedberg begin after the first month.

Dr. Hedberg: *"June 1 — dressing changed. There has been considerable further necrosis of the skin. We will have to remove some more.*

"June 2 — Further extensive loss of tissue was debrided under anesthesia. We may have to do a hemipelvectomy to get ahead of this thing. Disease — a real problem with sepsis and advancing gangrene. Please follow and advise." He was evidently addressing Dr. M.

The next notes were from Dr. M., the internist and infectious disease doctor, whom I remember seeing in my room but not in the operating room. *"June 4 — Shaking chills with temp to 101-plus this a.m. Unfortunately, abundant pseudomonas of two types, not surprising, but a most disturbing development."* Pseudomonas is the fast-spreading, flesh-eating bacteria more commonly called gangrene.

My mother recalls that the next day was an ordeal for everyone concerned. "After the operation, we were very apprehensive. Before you went into the next one Dr. Hedberg took me into his office and talked with me for a whole hour. He told me, 'I don't know how much we're going to have to take.' I said, 'What do you mean how much?' and he told me, 'I may have to take the torso.'

"I told him very hesitantly, 'That would be a terrible thing for her to handle...' You had heard them say something about what they might do, and you let me know you didn't want that. I didn't even know what a torso was," my mother admits, and I can't help but laugh, but I sober up quickly as she continues.

"He said, 'We might have to take an awful lot of her body, her buttock and hip.' I knew you'd feel terrible; they'd take a lot, and he'd feel terrible. After the operation he spoke with me another hour."

Especially difficult was the débridement. They were afraid to give me too much Ketamine — today far better anesthetics are available — so the doctors only gave me a local and débrided in my hospital room when they were — plain and simple — digging the remains of dead flesh out of the wound. The sensations would trigger any nerve in my pelvis, including my genitals.

The Ketamine, I'm told, was responsible for my hallucinations. I felt monkeys crawling all over me, tactile hallucinations, like snakes swirling around me, smothering me, and I would scream to get them off of me.

According to the nurse's notes, two weeks after the accident they performed the hemipelvectomy, and from June 9 through 16, débridement of the wound. The notes reveal it would be another week before they were sure the surgery was successful in saving my life, but they moved me from ICU to my own room.

The rest of the first three months I spent in a bed with a structure over me, like a wagon frame covered with a sheet — a big tent. I called it the Big Tent because so much pain went on underneath it I imagined a circus of sadists when they debrided the "wound." "Catching the gangrene" was the main event under the Big Tent. I never saw my body past my arms; the latter I would eventually exercise by lifting myself up on a triangle suspended above my head.

I don't want to dwell on what went on behind and beneath the tent, but it hurt like my insides were being scooped out of me. And they were. The doctors came in to débride the wound of its dead flesh; then came the nurses. Often, I yelled for them to stop hurting me — there — where no one should touch me without my permission.

Then there were the fevers, hot and cold, as my body shook and quaked as though I were on a bucking bronco. My mother would cry out, "Please help us, God!" Although I was a confirmed agnostic, I reiterated her prayer, believing from my Catholic catechism classes it would help to repeat it. Reading the hospital notes so I could reconstruct the first three weeks after my accident gave me the details of these tempests.

Once again the internist's notes, taken six full days after the last amputation, are the most descriptive of what went on in my hospital room immediately after I was under the Big Tent. "*June 11 — 2:30 p.m. Temperature to 105 with 45-minute shaking chill this p.m. Apparently no blood culture drawn, so...done tonight. She obviously has a sepsis focus capable of feeding bloodstream. Hopefully tomorrow's débridement will help."*

"*June 13 — Bad day...to 104-plus. Another attack this a.m. Sumps not working, has large painful mass on left flank. Culture results discouraging. Specimen sent out yesterday giving what appears to be almost pure culture of pseudomonas.*"

"*June 14 — She's flushed, febrile, uncomfortable, apparently sumps giving some problem again. Will have to be watched closely. June 15 — Pack beneath abdominal wall was causing a great deal of pain and tenderness and so was removed. Everything looks clean, temp is down to 100.*"

Another anesthesiologist leaves this note following the internist's: "*June 15. Anesthesia, massive pelvic trauma with packs and dressings to control losses. Circulation and gangrene now seem to be under control, but sepsis continues, with temp to 104 this p.m. Has had several exposures to Ketamine, which seems to be agent of choice for dressing change. Pathologist report not yet available — will almost certainly show pseudomonas vasculitis. June 16 — More débridement — 8 mg morphine 2 a.m.*"

Reading so many reports about débridement validated my memory that the débridement process was endless and felt as invasive as the surgeries.

Then, a note from Dr. Hedberg over a week after the hemipelvectomy amputation was performed signals there will be no more amputations necessary, only more débridement: *"The most encouraging dressing change to date. Only a speck of necrotic material on posterior wound edge. June 23 — Scheduled for further débridement. Miserable and depressed today — complaining of severe phantom pain."*

Internist's note: *"June 26 — After last night's episode, temp spike to 105 with rigor. She looks good again and has been afebrile today. Blood cultures are up in p.m. Later cultures of débridement material are growing abundant pseudomonas and (unfortunately) abundant yeast."*

The day I did my research at MGH and found the file from 1971, I couldn't wait to get home to read my copy of the transcripts, so I stopped into a café and previewed the doctor's notes. In the coffee shop I looked for the notes following the procedure most memorable to me. There is no mention of my psychological regression, and I am disappointed that the sensitive internist Dr. M. does not seem to have understood the psychological trauma of the event. But of course, he couldn't know the whole story.

The notes of the following months offer no hint of my emotional state, either, although they document a stabilization of the fever. No mention from Dr. A. or anyone, not even the nurses.

I will never forget the trauma of that last procedure. When Dr. Hedberg went on his summer vacation in August, they brought me down to lay the skin grafts over the huge gap, where all that separated my viscera from sepsis poisoning and death was a thin tissue of inner cavity fascia. It was the first time I was fully conscious in the O.R. No Ketamine, just a local anesthetic and a few valium before the operation.

"Please knock me out," I cried, looking up into the eyes of an older man who stood over my head. There were tears on both our parts.

Dr. A., who was standing in for Dr. Hedberg, dispassionately bore my cries of protest and proceeded with his work of slicing off a few more slabs of upper skin to finish the job. The rest of the skin for this procedure had been stored away from a previous harvesting. Unfortunately, this time I wasn't unconscious while the meat cutter made its whirring, slicing sounds collecting slabs of skin tissue to lie on the wound. I imagined what it would feel like, and I felt my own imaginations. Later, when she saw the condition of my emotions after the surgery, my mother screamed at Dr. A. for not sedating me enough.

"Do you know what this girl has been through? Are you some kind of monster? How dare you take her down there with nothing but a light medication? She needs a real doctor, who cares," she hissed, "not a robot who can't imagine what it would be like to go down to those operating rooms where she suffered so much, and for her to be awake and aware." I can't remember if she used the word torture, but she implied it.

"I stand corrected. I stand corrected," Dr. A. repeated woodenly, backing up against the wall as my mother hissed in response to my regressed state returning to my hospital bed.

"I'm just a little baby. I'm just a little baby," I cried over and over and over again. I remember even now saying it, and not being sure why, but feeling I must say it.

What may have pushed me over the edge beyond the anguish of the procedure was that they left me outside the operating room for dispatch to take me upstairs. After a while, I felt cold air on my body as the sheet covering me was lifted. Because my eyes were closed, some person thought I was unconscious. I heard him say almost furtively, "Look at this." It wasn't a gasp; it was a horrible silence that wouldn't tell me if they were still there or had moved on, until I felt the sheet back over me. No longer protected by The Big Tent, utterly humiliated, I was afraid to open my eyes. I was indeed helpless, exploited and shamed and that feeling did not go away for a long time.

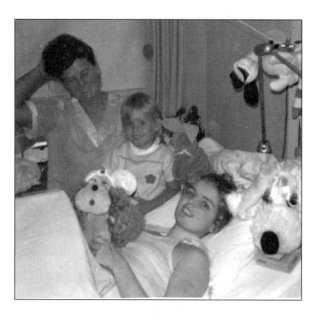

Top: 1971. My mother and a neighbor girl she was babysitting visit me and my plush menagerie around the "Big Tent." Bottom: 1971. Nurse Jean Donovan.

Damage Done

(Chapter 6, Miss American Pie)

In late June, after a month of fighting for my life, half in the ICU and half under the Big Tent in Baker 10, I was considered "recovering." But as the sun and humidity of July in New England heated up my single private hospital room, I began to feel worse. For the first time I could remember, I couldn't run away from emotional pain, nor could I deny it, because it found expression in my body.

I was sensitive to tension and anything negative. Vietnam War footage on the nightly news psychically gagged me. If a show on the television above my bed portrayed anything remotely supernatural, like a show called Dr. Phibes, or was violent, I had to click it off before it swarmed my nervous system, before the pressure built up in the hot, burning pain in my now-absent left foot, making it feel like it was going to burst. My leg wasn't there anymore, but the nerve endings were. Most amputees have the pins-and-needle sensation called phantom limb. However, it was my great misfortune to be one of the two to three percent of amputees who have chronic pain from the nerve damage. Even the overhead fan that recycled the room's stifled air exacerbated the sensation known as "phantom pain."

Unfortunately, the fan could not displace the tension in the air as my mother's protectiveness clashed with the different nurses. My leftist mother found a comfortable political groove with my special-duty, Latvian born nurse, Ehva, until the latter gave an impassioned speech about zero population growth, declaring that people who had more than two children were selfish and irresponsible. My mother, who converted to Catholicism by marriage, reacted as though struck. A heated argument ensued without my mother mentioning the fact of our family's size. If only Ehva knew that my mother had borne eight children in ten years, I thought, not because she wanted that many (my father was mentally ill and often couldn't keep a job), but because she and her Catholic husband followed the church's lead on the practice of birth control. Never mind that when she tried to leave him, her own father wouldn't allow her and her three children to come home to her mother's house. He followed the "You made your bed; now lie in it" school of tough luck.

For myself, I couldn't imagine my family without the little kids, Stephen, Joanne and Susie. Even Timothy John and Kathleen, who were dead now, were part of our family. I wasn't a good Catholic, but my sympathy was with my mother.

I was happiest when the special-duty nurse, Jean Donovan, was there. She was the one nurse who really liked my mother and one of the few for whom my mother returned the feeling. She was extraordinarily professional while at the same time compassionate and personal with me.

Jeannie came in at 7 a.m. and practiced her birdcalls. I imagined her whispery whistles of wind were passed through her lips in a memory of what the bird looked like. There was nary a parakeet within one mile of my room, so I loved this habit of hers. It was one of the few ways the natural world reached me, I was so sealed off in that stuffy, single, corner room I inhabited during the sweltering summer of '71.

Daily my mother swept into my hospital room, bringing a bright, cheery countenance and some new item to make my world better. With her spray bottle of a popular fragrance called "Love's Lemon Fresh," she transformed the molecules of antiseptic hospital air and the putrid smell of gangrenous flesh from my débridement that hovered over the Big Tent. She whirled in like a bright, yellow, sparkling tornado spraying the room, and bringing me news of the other patients on the floor, on whom she had dropped in before she arrived.

My mother got the Love's Lemon Fresh from a young woman down the hall who was recovering from breast reduction surgery. The young woman came in to visit me because my mother told her it would make me feel better to know I wasn't the only teenager on Baker 10 that summer. My mother thought we would find something to talk about, both of our losses in the domain of the female. However, I could not relate to my new visitor who had elected a surgery to reduce her female "stuff," while I felt surgery had stolen mine; I was too damaged to meet a new friend.

My mother, an incorrigible optimist, was at her best around pessimists like my father. Given a scarcity of these, her next best challenge was a person in pain or misery of the transient kind, for which the hospital was a repository. She made friends, for instance, with the young man in traction whose family lived in Connecticut, stopping in to see him every day. She befriended the woman dying of esophageal cancer and told me all about the woman's struggles, no doubt, to contrast my survival and demonstrate my advantage.

After the audience of interns and residents who had been trained under the Big Tent diminished, my only other regular visitor besides my mother and the nurses was Dr. Hedberg. My feelings for him at the time were too complicated to say I had come to care for him, but I missed him if he didn't stop by. It wasn't until the next summer that I would realize the extent of his caring for me.

When he strode down the hallways at Mass General Hospital, heads turned; the nurses called him "Little Stevie Wonder." Dr. Steven Hedberg, Harvard Medical School graduate and oncology surgeon, was a wunderkind of medicine at 42. Very tall, handsome and brutally honest, he was assigned to me with my pelvic injuries because he had done radical female amputations on women who had in some cases little chance of surviving their cancer in spite of the amputations. I suspect he thought I was lucky because, with the gangrene gone, I was out of the woods.

When he came in to débride the amputation site, I always screamed at him to stop. It felt like he was scraping away the parts of me that hurt so much when a girl rides a boy's bicycle and falls onto the bar. He seemed not to notice, he was so focused on his task. Jeannie, on the other hand, was concerned after I chastised her for hurting me in my private parts — which I thought were still there. She expressed her fear and frustration about not knowing what she was seeing down in the gore where my perineal platform, the crotch between two legs, had been. Was that "opening" the urethra, the vagina or the rectum? He spoke to her gruffly. "Go to the ladies room; get out your mirror and take a good look. Come back after you figure it out."

I remember that I was obsessed with the roll of film I had dropped off at the drug store in Amherst just before our fatal drive. When I finally got the photographs back, I was hit hard by the images. The first photo showed five girls linked arm to arm in front of our dormitory. I was wearing a long red calico dress my roommate Bobby had sewed for me. Another picture focused on all of our feet kicking out from under the red calico skirt. We were doing an ankles-down can-can. When I saw those pictures I knew exactly how we were feeling. It was a happy farewell we were performing as we took these last photos; it would be autumn before we would all see each other again.

The other three pictures were more poignant. In one, I was wearing my bathing suit top and cut-off short-shorts preparing to perform a cartwheel, both arms and my right leg raised in the air. In another, Mark waded in a pond, his jeans rolled up, sun lighting up his lean, rippling back and chest muscles, and I lounged in the foreground on a rock, facing the camera. The beauty of the day was brought back to me with these images. The photographs were all I had left of Mark, all I had left to remind me of my lost self.

I was pierced with anger and loss, and I demanded to see Dr. Hedberg.

He eventually came, summoned by nurses. Holding the pictures in one hand, I pointed at the cartwheel pose.

"Do you see who I was? Do I look like that now? Do you see what you've done?" I was so angry, on the verge of tears. "Why didn't you just throw me in the barrel with everything else you took?" I demanded.

He looked down at me, tucking his chin in. "That's your problem," he told me from his serene advantage. "I just had to save your life. Now you have to do the rest." He talked on with the passion of a poker player.

"You can take a gun," he held his finger against his temple, "and do whatever you need to do. My job was to save your life." I hated his composure and his glib answers. When I asked him if I could still bear children, he didn't answer yes or no, but, "Without a pelvis to hold them in, sure. They'll tumble out."

After my eighth week under the Big Tent, he asked me if I had taken a look at myself. "No," I told him, shocked at the suggestion.

"Well, what are you waiting for?"

"I'll do it," I said, grudgingly, staring over the top of the Big Tent, actually surprised he was expecting this of me. "Gradually."

"What are you going to do, put seven veils over it?" was his response.

One day Jeannie moved the sheet off the frame of the Big Tent and held a mirror for me to look at the amputation site. I was protected by edges of the mirror, which caught mainly the reflection of the area they called "the wound." It's hard to describe what I saw in the mirror. I could not see the whole, huge chunk of body that felt butchered off, but I saw its absence.

I think of the John Donne poem, "No man is an island; every man is a part of the continent, a piece of the main. If a clod bee [sic] washed away by the sea," Donne wrote, "Europe would bee [sic] the less." One quarter of my body was the "clod" washed away by the sea. This was my first glimpse of the new continent.

Had I not endured seemingly endless seconds, minutes, hours, days and weeks of pain, I might not have believed my eyes. Although my whole hip, buttock, and crotch were gone, and an ugly, open red space stared back at me in the mirror, I could still feel my missing body parts in the poking, burning phantom pain. I quickly looked away, and Jeannie put the cover back on.

For months I had crowded my right hip to the right side of the bed when the doctors came in with their circus of surgeon tricks to débride under the Big Tent, and they directed me to shift my body to the left. I had always been afraid my left side would touch the railings. The reality was that below my waist, I had no left side anymore. I now saw this.

Where was my sex? I didn't want to look further, but I had seen it — gone.

There was some pubic hair down there on the right side where I still had half a pubis, but the inside had been scooped out; and there was not a corresponding mons on the left. As a good Catholic girl, I knew the clitoris and hymen from scandalous books like Mary McCarthy's *The Group*. These were the only internal parts for which I had a name, however mispronounced. Years later I would not only learn the names but also study the anatomy intimately by reading the same published articles in medical books about female pelvic floor disorders that the specialists read to prepare for reconstructive surgeries like my own.

My vantage point this day was far different; I couldn't even see what was gone by looking on the right for the correspondent part. On the left, no hip, no groin, no mons. Without the mons, no protective guard. Nothing. Could I really be gone beyond the center? I didn't know it then because I didn't touch myself. But I would find out when I finally had the courage to touch myself that there was no spongy, soft clitoris; no hymen left to break, no nothing. Not even any soft labia, thin and full of promise.

I felt an inky, heavy slowing down and pooling of blood as if I were being poisoned and watching. I next felt a rush to what I believed was my center, but of course it wasn't there; I had a new center. What *was* there was a cavity, with a catheter sticking out of my left side from what must have been my urethra. It looked like just another drainage hose siphoning off the infection.

My breath slowed until I had to swallow it and let in the new breath. This breath carried emotion from my belly to the back of my throat pushing out, pushing out, trying to push out the feeling I couldn't name.

My grainy phantom leg throbbing, I leaned over the bed for the phone and dialed my mother. When she answered the phone, she knew right away this was the call.

I was sobbing, and I hiccuped in the draw of these breaths, "So, you know what they did to me, Ma?" I was shaking and couldn't hold onto the phone anymore, so Jean put the phone on the pillow, in this half-raised hospital bed with scratchy, starched sheets, and then she left the room. Resting my arms to the right side of the Big Tent, I leaned into the phone, tears falling into the hollow of my chin against the receiver, and I cried to my mother, "Did you see what they did to me? They took my body."

The cries came out of me in a whine, like my breath was a bow and my body the violin, the sound changing its timbre and intensity with some felt dirge inside me.

"This is what they took, Ma?" I was sobbing uncontrollably, tears coursing like an overflowing river. Deep-crying breaths followed. Was each exhalation clearing out the cells, organs and limbs to have room for this new knowledge? There must be some reason for your body to cry when your mind doesn't want it to.

"Carolyn?" Her voice was very quiet. She used my childhood name.

"Did you see it?" It wasn't outrage like I had felt with Dr. Hedberg about the photographs. It was just horror looking for an answer or some understanding, possibly a "say it ain't so." The saying, "beside oneself with grief" implies some splitting. There was no splitting; it was all there, all of my grief as if from a well in my body whose depth wasn't physical; its depth was centuries worth of dying, of losing, of crying out for it not to be true. Please don't let it be true; don't let it be real; why can't it be a dream?

"Did you see how much they took?" I moved into anger. Anger at her. "How can I live like this?" I demanded. "They took my whole body." And the wound. How could it be called that? It was like a mine gouged in a mountainside, no trees, grass, water, just dirt and digging and lines of blood vessels popping out of the grafts they had taken from my right thigh and my left thoracic wall to cover the crevice.

"I know, dear. I know." There is no describing the emotion my mother could convey with her voice: She knew.

Later, she shared with me what I vaguely remembered once she reminded me. I asked her if she remembered me telling them I didn't want them to do that amputation where they would take more than my leg. I asked her how Dr. Hedberg felt after the surgery.

She sighed heavily. "Oh, he'd taken a terrible lot out of you. He was pleased with the surgery."

I knew she meant he was satisfied that he had gone far enough to catch the gangrene. But why hadn't she asked him if I could still have sex? If I could still have children? Had she admitted the whole thing to herself yet? Or was it not something she felt comfortable talking about with him, nor with me later? If it weren't for her report about the operating room, I wouldn't have thought sex or orgasm was possible.

My mother described Dr. Hedberg's state of mind which she considered inseparable from my survival. "The anesthesia man came up to see you afterward, but Dr. Hedberg felt so bad, he couldn't see you. You had a healthy, beautiful body, and it meant a lot to you. He knew because you had told him. When you did see him, you said, 'I told you not to take my torso, now throw the rest of me away,' and that's when he told you it was his job to save you. If you wanted to take your own life, you needed to do that for yourself. That seemed to satisfy you."

"Did I know during the last surgery what was happening?" I asked. I realize writing this what a foolish question that was. How can anyone know "what was happening" under anesthesia?

"You were quoting Camus and the existentialists," my mother said, "and he told you, 'I like Sartre,' and then you said Sartre was too cynical for you." My mother went on with uncharacteristic candor regarding my "vulgar" tongue to recreate the conversations that I had had in the operating room under a full general anesthetic.

"You said, 'Who's going to want me without my body?' and several of the doctors — and that young, handsome, Dr. Ryan was there — said, 'Well, I wouldn't throw you out of bed!' "

I do recall, as her testimony reminds me, asking the doctors how was I going to be called a "nice piece of ass" anymore. I couldn't articulate the pun the way it really was witty, which was, "Now they literally can call me a piece of ass." So sexually naive, I didn't fully realize that this expression meant having had a girl, sexually. I foolishly thought when the boys said that to you it was a compliment based on how your rear end looked in blue jeans.

Dr. Hedberg was shocked a year later to hear that I had been a virgin. I told him then, "You're the one who took away my virginity."

After my infamous line about piece of ass, my mother told me the doctors then said, "You still have beautiful breasts." I'm sure it was a consolation only a man could appreciate, and one which my mother heard with mixed feelings, considering she disapproved of men talking about parts of women's bodies objectively. Even as objects d'art. My mother was so modest she would blush to find a statue with its breasts bared.

Later, after the intern's comments about my breasts, my mother said, "Don't worry, dear, there are other kinds of love," and then, in her words, "And then that young, handsome Dr. Ryan spoke up for you. 'Don't you ever say that to her. She can have intercourse.' " True. I still had one and a half inches of vaginal canal left, and there was always the good old accommodating vagina at the cervix to make more room for a man. But they had left me no pudenda, nor clitoris.

We never talked about "my amputation" being a sexual loss, but all along, my mother had been aware of the magnitude of the last surgery. Implicit at the time was that this loss was worth the exchange for my life. Except for that one time, this trade-off was not discussed with me in terms of either a loss of sexual function or sexual feeling. The amputation was referred to in terms of the loss of bone — hemipelvectomy.

Several months after I left the hospital, in Dr. Hedberg's office, I released my need to address my surgery in this way: I charged him, "You castrated me."

"I didn't castrate you; you can only do that to a man," he retorted with his usual dry expression. I sat on the counter of his examining room, speechless; I thought to myself, totally at a loss, they don't even have a word for it with women. I knew people had lost legs before, but I never thought that losing this much body was possible, and I was trying to understand.

I hardly understand now.

My mother's recollection about the amputations makes the operating room out to be a place of almost lighthearted banter, but my body's memory is different. To this day I have nightmares of physical annihilation, my body pulverized to ash. For four years after a new reconstructive pelvic surgery, I couldn't sleep. My body's memory had been triggered, and every time I was about to lose consciousness — even in a lying-down daydream — I would awake before I could fall into a daze, terrified that someone might hurt me in my sleep.

I learned only several years ago that vulvectomies are not wholly unusual in the United States. Performed on women in the advanced stages of vulvular cancer, the process of reconstruction is, I'm sure, more clean and sophisticated than in a trauma case like mine. Years later, I asked the doctor who was scheduled to do my second

Top: my hospital room wall. Bottom: circa 1960, Revere Beach Boulevard. If you look carefully, you can see the double Ferris wheel in the background.

reconstruction, who told me about vulvectomies, if I could speak to one of his patients who'd had the procedure. He hesitated, and then told me few had lived. I wonder if spending the last years of your life living with this pain and loss are worth the exchange — for those who live that long.

For me, it has been worth it to live. I would discover in the course of my new life the degree to which I would enjoy my sexuality. However, at the time I first saw the extent of the damage done, being a sexy young woman was not an option anymore. I dealt with the initial shock of seeing my amputation for the first time by numbing myself to my body.

In my hospital room at night, the four walls closed in on me like a tomb; the glittering get-well cards activated by the fan waved out eerily to me. I felt my left leg and the rest of the damage done to my pelvis as though the lost parts were encased in amber, like a bug or a fossil. They were still a part of me, yet unreal, fixed in the resin of the past and the body's neural memory.

1971. Mark's mother, Dottie, and her youngest son, Glenn.

First Leg of the Journey
(Chapter 12, Miss American Pie)

I had referred to independence so often as standing on my own two feet, it only seemed logical to now pursue an artificial leg. On more than one level that first leg was a kick in the pants.

I knew nothing of prosthetics before the accident, but I had no trouble picturing my artificial limb. When they told me at Cooly Dickenson Hospital, "Cale, we're going to have to take your leg," I remember picturing a doll-like limb I would set against the wall inside my door in the basement dorm room I was coveting for my sophomore year residence. I must've expected I'd be really on the go with it, right next to the door — the doorknob side, no less. The leg in this fantasy was made of rubber, like a doll's. It had a foot with a high arch like mine and well-developed calves like mine — though I wouldn't mind if the thigh was skinnier — like Barbie's thighs.

Then, I imagined walking to the beach, down to the water's edge on a foot with artistically designed toes to match my own painted-pink live ones, only these would not get cold. I'd just stand there, sinking down into the sand while the tide came in, much like a beach chair oblivious to the ocean's warning. I could stand there for a while like a flamingo not getting my other foot wet, I imagined. The look of my prosthetic fantasy was life-like, seamless, like a doll's when you take her to the doll hospital. When I was a kid I thought a doll hospital was a place where real doctors performed real live miracle healing on dolls; they don't super glue at a doll hospital, I was sure. Maybe they designed a life-like rubber sleeve to keep the leg on you; it would fit seamlessly over the ridge where your own and the artificial leg meet. This area is called a stump in real life.

So when they said, "Cale, we're going to take part of your torso," I cried and said no.

You could replace a body part like a leg, but not a part of a body part like a hip or pelvis, a buttock or pubic bone, or whatever else was in a torso, I wasn't sure. I didn't think of logistical things like weight-bearing, since no doll had to worry about that; she walked when you walked her. Swing-through, weight-bearing, circumducting and hyperextending, all the nuts-and-bolts realities of physical therapy and gait-training, these I couldn't have imagined ahead of time.

The first time I went to a prosthetist, my eyes opened so wide I couldn't close them to sleep for a week. The psychiatric social worker from the hospital took me there in a taxi, and I was glad I wasn't alone. I expected the white-walled, white-linoleum-clean of a clinic, and was shocked enough to get out of the cab at a street called Columbus Avenue, famous for its whores, pimps, drug dealers and winos on the doorsteps. We entered the corner building into a darkly paneled interior with a high wood counter, behind which an older woman sat typing until she heard a bell ring and the door pushed shut.

She motioned us to sit, after handing us a clipboard and forms to fill out. I didn't know what to write when they asked what type my amputation was. "Hemipelvectomy," Jane prompted me.

The first prosthetist met me in the waiting room and ushered me to one of half a dozen six-by-twelve-foot cubicles whose privacy was protected with burlap curtains at the portals. He instructed me to lie down on the leather-upholstered table and, after drawing an outline of my body on a large piece of paper, advised me he'd be right back.

"Gil, we've got a radical hemi here I need you to take a look at," I heard him shout as he entered the back room. I looked at Jane, who wasn't much more than five years older than I. She was looking at me as if to see what I was thinking. I raised both my eyebrows at her as if to say, "Why hasn't anyone called me a 'radical' hemi before this? An MGH conspiracy? I have to come here to find out I'm radical?"

Gil came out with a canvas apron, sawdust and other particulates mashed against his lap. He was younger than the other gray-haired man, dark wavy hair, perhaps of Italian descent. He explained they were going to make the bucket part of my leg.

"What's the "bucket?" I asked.

"The way hemipelvectomies are fitted with limbs is for a bucket to bear the weight thoracically," said the first prosthetist.

"Thoracically? What's that?"

"That's your rib cage," he started to explain, and I started to panic.

"You didn't ask for any x-rays. I don't have all my ribs…I-I-lost a floater rib…" I looked at Jane Cartwright.

"Cale, your orthopedic surgeon wrote you a prescription. I'm sure he knows about your rib," Jane Cartwright tried to reassure me, but I was getting nervous.

"Can I see one of these hemipelvectomy legs?" I asked, looking around the cubicle, knowing full well there wasn't anything but furniture and a plant in the space.

"We don't have any hemis here, but next visit we'll have the bucket made. The bucket is where the prosthesis wraps around you, and we attach the leg below the bucket."

It sounded so ugly, so confining, like a chastity belt, was all I could think. Six months earlier, I had entertained the picture of my torso thrown away in a trashcan by Dr. Hedberg, but this was a whole new twist. Anyway, how could a bucket wrap around you? It was all so hard to imagine.

I was glad my mother wasn't there. She'd know both what I was thinking and feeling. Who knew what she might do?! Demand some respect, or something. I was always embarrassed when my mother launched into an impassioned speech about how our government spent more money researching travels in space than it did in developing better ways for people to live here on earth. I knew I wouldn't be able to lean on my mother much longer, so this was a dry run for what it would be like at the University Infirmary, where the MGH's discharge team had made sure I was in contact for my transition back to school. But I was very glad I had another woman with me when I heard what this guy Gil was going to do with me.

The prosthetist came back with two long, skinny pieces of cotton knit tubing that had been sewn at an angle from the bottom, so, as from Florida's southern tip north to the mainland, the stockinette's design jutted out to be wider at the top, say from Louisiana's easternmost border to the coast of Georgia.

"Take off all your clothes except your bra, and then pull both of these stockinets on up to your chest," instructed the first prosthetist. I took the first layer of stockinet, put my leg into the mainland and then stepped into the peninsula, pulling the top of Florida up to my crotch, the mainland up to my chest, with Louisiana and the Georgia coast around my waist. My toes probably in Cuba by now, I lost my balance. Jane Cartwright caught me and helped me stand up to put on the second one. Then we waited.

Both men arrived, this time wearing white coats and pants, and Gil carried a pail of water and several rolls of some unidentified ribbon. This he soon informed me was just how they make the "mold" before they can make the leg. The ribbon was actually strips of plaster of Paris. While the other man wrapped me in the ribbon, Gil, starting above my waist, began watering down the plaster with his hands. I watched his large, competent hands, not as delicate or smooth as a doctors, and his dark, hairy forearms as he rubbed in smooth strokes around my lower torso, making sure he covered the strips evenly until he reached the lower panty leg portion of my right hip and readied to pass over my amputation site.

Squatting on his haunches, he stopped momentarily. He was a little perturbed because the urinary catheter was not something they usually had to contend with in making casts. Neither was the leg bag, but at least that he didn't have to cover. He asked if we could take it out, but we couldn't.

It was most disconcerting. I couldn't cry, I couldn't whine, I couldn't protest. This was yet another experience of the body I had to psychically step away from, or risk tripping

61

over an emotional live wire. I did not want him rubbing my body like that.

It seemed like it was just as hard for Gil to have to perform this plaster job. He was appropriately embarrassed when he got to my crotch, which made me appreciate him a little. But I immediately stiffened when he told me that the plaster would get warm, and then we'd have to wait until it cooled and hardened. For 15 minutes I didn't look at or say anything to Jane; I just stood there frozen until the other man came back with a silver, rotating power saw with teeth that made this instrument more terrifying than the dentist drill. Fortunately, unlike the dentist drill, it didn't hurt. First Gil drew a plumb line down the front of the now-hardened plaster cast with a fat, red crayon.

He touched the tip of the saw's teeth to the surface of the plaster and turned on the loud, whirring instrument. My body kept shrinking from the saw in a natural protective response he did not discourage. When he'd cut a few inches he put his hand inside the plaster mold between the two layers of stockinet and seemed pleased he had not cut through the second layer of cotton knit, which hugged my clammy skin. Then he went on with his whirring, which might not have been so nauseating if it hadn't reminded me of the whirring meat cutter they used for my skin grafts. When he got too close to my skin, the saw screeched shrilly, and he adjusted the pressure. When he was done, I stood there exhausted, barely able to stand even while holding onto the table and Jane holding my elbows.

"Just one more step," he announced, and he proceeded to widen the opening enough to pull the cast away from my body, and then he twisted and lowered it down my torso where I thought he might open it up enough to pull it around my leg. Instead, he protected it by having me sit down. He then pulled it off deliberately, like a bathing suit full of sand you're trying not to spill on the floor. I watched him gingerly carry this strange piece of plaster with fabric hanging from both ends in the shape of nothing I'd ever seen before. I watched after it, stupefied. Of course, it was the shape of my new body. Venus de Milo's latest troubles.

The taxi came to pick us up after we'd set the date for my next appointment, and when we got inside, I could no longer hold back the tears. "I hate that place. I don't want to go back," I pronounced when I could get my tears under control.

Jane said, "Just a few more times for the fittings. You did really well." She was a psychologist and a social worker; she must have had many observations and insights, but she wasn't going to share them with me.

The next day in doctor's rounds at Bullfinch, the psychiatric floor of MCH, everyone asked me eagerly how my visit to the brace clinic went — like I'd been to Disneyland or something.

"It wasn't a clinic," I corrected them, through clenched teeth. "It was a sweat shop."

Just before I went back to school I had my second visit to the "brace shop." This time I noticed more detail. No wonder they called it that; one look in the window and you had to brace yourself to walk in the door. The shop windows were haphazardly arrayed with various artificial limbs — legs, arms and hands, and ugly metal and leather extensions that people wore god-knows-where on their bodies. How could they even display these instruments of cruelty? No wonder the winos were all passed out on the sidewalk.

Inside, this time the receptionist knew my name and called through an intercom to another room for the Prosthetist Number One. He met me, brought us to a cubicle, and we sat there for half an hour before he came in with the hard plastic bucket, which looked like petrified ladies' briefs only higher at the waist, lower at the leg, and with leather straps and buckles in the front. It was the latter that pushed me to tears. But because we had an agenda, he just said, "Now, there," and "Stand up now, and we'll try this on you."

Leather straps and buckles? How would I wear my dress over that thing, never mind my tighter jerseys and blouses. Forget midriff shirts. It was bad enough they took away half my body, but now they were going to ruin the effects of what was left. Bye, Bye, Miss American Pie. I could hear that song again. All the drive, hope and ambition drained out of me while he pulled the plastic as tightly as he could and fumbled with the straps to get them to hold me there. I hadn't seen it with the leg attached, but already I hated it. When he told me to try sitting down, it cut into me at the crease in my thigh at my good right hip; and under my rectum and vagina, it cut into me in an excruciating manner.

"Now, it's not going to feel right at first. That's why we have fittings. You have to tell me what bothers you, so we can make adjustments."

"When's it going to have a leg?" I asked irritably, getting up from the sitting position as quickly as I could, struggling for control of my emotions. I wanted to tear the thing off.

"Well, first we have to get the bucket right."

"Why do they have to call it a bucket?" I whined. "Who wants to wear a bucket, sit in a pail?" I wanted to tell him how stupid it all was, but I waited and told it to the nurses at the hospital when I returned. In the taxi, I told Jane Cartwright I wasn't going back; but I knew I would have to sooner or later. Later would be two weeks after school started, when I was scheduled to return to the hospital for a short visit to make sure school was going okay and that it was right for me to be back at UMass.

The first visit after they made modifications on the bucket based on my fitting, I expected the bucket to fit my body better. Yet when I took it off, I noticed the plastic had cut into my rectum where I sat and left a smudge of blood. I was so embarrassed thinking maybe they'd think my period left its mark, but no one said anything.

Gil came back from making a few more changes, and this time wanted to know how it fit "down there." I put my finger to the places that hurt, Gil took a closer look, and with his fat red pencil made marks along the floor of the bucket's platform. "I'll be right back," he said, and he disappeared into the workroom of the prosthetic shop, leaving the door slightly ajar.

While he was away, I got up, and, not unlike Toto pulling the curtain away from the smoke and mirrors illusion of the Wizard of Oz, I stole a look at the shop behind the door. There was my torso, cast in plaster, skewered vertically by an iron rod and anchored horizontally on a vise. The vise fit on a carousel mounted perpendicularly to the floor. I was surprised to see sewing machines and white dust everywhere. When I saw Gil look up from one of the machines, I shut the door quickly and sat back up on the table. When I closed my eyes I thought of Dastardly Dan and the maiden tied up and pulled inexorably to the circular saw in the infamous cartoon.

When he returned, the crotch was cut almost entirely out of the bucket.

"That's better," I said and hoped we were done, still in shock over the mess of limb shapes I'd just seen in plaster. However, he had to measure my good leg from heel to knee, knee to hip, so I had to wait some more. When I left the prosthetic shop this time, I was angry with myself for having hope. This was no doll hospital.

That night I dreamed I was a robot, armored and wired — except my head was missing. I realized I was at a party, and I felt very out of place, so I went looking for my head so I could leave. I found my head. She was on the bed with the coats, and I picked her up by her curly blonde hair from the back. When I brought her toward me, my head was smiling, having just had a good laugh, and looked like I was having a wonderful time. I didn't even bother putting her back on my shoulders. I just grabbed my coat and carried my coat and my head away from the party.

In two days, I had the final fitting of the week, the first of many fittings before the leg part of the prosthesis was walkable. My anxiety was great, but when I remembered my dream, I had a good laugh at myself. I didn't laugh my head off or anything, but I did recognize that after breakfast in the morning, when it was time to go into town for my leg appointment, I had run around like a chicken with her head cut off. I couldn't find my keys, my jacket, and then couldn't find the pair of pants I was going to try on with my new leg.

The advances in prosthetics over the past 30 years are enormous, yet minuscule for hemipelvectomies. Prosthetists can make arms for people, then physical therapists train them how to control the fingers electronically with their own brains, yet they can't make a light enough knee for a hemipelvectomy that could keep the artificial leg's weight under 12 pounds! That's not 12 pounds like the live 12 of 22 my body lost in the accident, but 12 pounds of dead weight that my now less-abled body, specifically with a spine weakened by the imbalance in the pelvis, had to activate.

And the knee is not all a hemi needs in prosthetic parts, but a hip joint, an ankle and a foot, as well. The joints are all extremely sensitive to angles and degrees of rotation, so they must be fine-tuned endlessly. You walk back and forth along a short walkway while the prosthetist asks you questions that make the eye doctor's, "this one? or this one?" seem like a simpleton's concerns.

But it wasn't the weight, the adjustments or any of the mechanics that consumed me with angst that first day after I tried on a pair of pants. I was pleased to see my shoe under the pant leg partnered up with the other one again, but it was the rear end that had me confounded. Where was the hip and butt on the left side? My pants just "slipped" down that side. My right hip was more pronounced because of how tightly the buckled plastic cinched in my waist. But on the left side, the "bucket" — just like a pail — straight up and down, with nothing to really hold the pants on like women's hips usually do. And it caved in where my buttock obviously wasn't. I pointed this out to them, but they weren't concerned with that as much as with how I sat with it.

So I sat, and I saw now that, with the leg attachment beneath one side of the bucket, I was pushed upward on my left. So we did more fittings. I pointed out again that I needed some kind of shape to make the left rear of my pant leg fill out in the back, and hold up my pants.

They returned half an hour later, this time with a block of cork about the size of the heel of a shoe glued to the back of the bucket so that it pushed out the fabric to give a facsimile of shape while also raising that side. I didn't try to further convince them of the importance of what I later learned is called "cosmesis of the prosthesis." I was horrified.

"It looks like somebody kicked me in the pants and left half their shoe there," I cried bitterly to my mother. I tried wearing it a few times, but after a few trials I really lost all hope of wearing a leg and did exactly what Dr. Hedberg said hemipelvectomies do: I threw it in the closet. I was now a monoped

1976, Sunapee, NH. Cover of NE Handicapped Sports brochure

The Adventures

Relaxing with a margarita at Maria's, outside Garafon, in Isla Mujeres, an island off Cancún, Mexico. The north end of the island, Garafon, is Jacques Cousteau's favorite place to snorkel.

The following stories are arranged chronologically in the sequence they were experienced, not written. Some chapters are essays from the newspaper and magazines for which I wrote my first columns. For these chapters, I include the name of the original publication and date of reprints. Because each was written for a different audience and purpose, there will be some repetition of facts.

1981, Arches National Park, Utah. Hiking is tough on hands and shoulders, but the spectacular view is worth it. Photo by Joanne Yankovich.

Gamble in Vegas

(1995 *Howlings*)

I walked a mile down the Grand Canyon and then back up again. That's two miles of crutch walking, which, if you think about it, is like vaulting over portable parallel bars.

The night of phantom limb pain that followed was an ordeal, but the next day made up for it, when, at a treeless KOA campground outside Las Vegas, I met a handsome biker riding a Suzuki 1000. He told me he'd had his eardrums blown out in Vietnam and his vision blurred by a shell blast, putting him in the ranks of disabled American veterans. He was sensitive to my amputation, aware because so many veterans lost limbs in the war. We talked, and he asked me if I wanted to go for a ride. I hesitated. This is how I lost my leg. I told him to let me think about it.

I went immediately to the bathroom, sat on a seat, and while staring at the timeless graffiti, I weighed the pros and cons.

Haven't you had enough excitement this week climbing down the largest canyon in the world?

Well, yes, but...Wouldn't it be great to see the countryside from a motorcycle again? Wouldn't it be a good thing to break that taboo and get back in the saddle?

But what if something happened again?

Do you know the odds of something like that happening again?

And if something did happen, it would be against all the odds. Only you would be a real loser.

I didn't feel like a loser, and somehow, maybe because I was so near Las Vegas, this idea of the odds made sense. It lent some logic to my calculations.

Okay. Think it through: It's a large motorcycle, built for highway cruising — nothing like the 350 BSA street bike Mark and I were on when we were hit head-on four years ago.

But what about his blurring vision?

Hey, he made it this far, didn't he?

Yes, but . . . do you trust him?

He promised to be really aware of me back there and to stop if I have any nerves or doubts. He knows trauma. I can only hope he'll be as sensitive as he seems.

Well, at least this time you know what can happen.

"Here I sit brokenhearted. Came to shit and only farted," the graffiti stared back. For the first time, these words struck me as both poetic and poignant statements about life. I didn't just come to see Vegas, I came to experience it!

Go for it, I thought. Okay, I'll tempt fate — this time, however, with much caution, extracting promises from my driver that there was enough of a seat for me to balance on, and that he would pull the bike over the minute I got scared.

Helmeted, holding on for dear life, I was taken on an excursion to the Hoover Dam. The rush of air and scenery were familiar and still intoxicating, but I knew now that I didn't need to do this again.

Once there, judging the wide expanse of terrain we'd have to cover in the dam's interior, he shanghaied a wheelchair from the people who give tours of the huge water facility, and he drove me in mock recklessness around my week's second amazing wonder of the world. I was smitten by his tenderness and attention to my circumstance.

Later, we drove home through the traffic on one of Vegas' teeming main streets. I caught a look at myself in the reflection of a glass building in the late-afternoon sun.

Mini-skirted, my strong, tanned leg gripping the body of the bike, my cleavage winking through a denim halter, I looked out from my right side and saw an image of any other glamorous gal on a motorbike. My blonde hair shining, streaking outside the helmet, I smiled at myself in the mirror. I looked . . . intact.

But in the shadows, on the left side, no companion leg straddled the seat, just my trusty wooden crutches, strapped horizontally the length of the bike.

This was the side of me I didn't feel that day.

Carolimb, shown from the back and shown on me as I pose at the Tuileries, took me on many adventures, including one to Paris and Amsterdam.

LIfe with Carolimb

(1979 *Caleidescope, Winter Park Manifest*)

Not many people have the misfortune, or privilege — however you feel about it — to own and operate an artificial appendage. But those who do, through design or default, are privy to a few "different" experiences in life that can sometimes fall into the category of humorous.

For amputees, prosthetics is not just another dirty word, nor a dirty profession, just an expensive and tongue-tripping name for that counterfeit "thing" that we strap onto our otherwise healthy bodies to take the place of that one, two, or more fleshy outgrowths called limbs that we have somehow managed to lose in our lifetimes. Or temporarily misplace, if you believe the Christian Scientists that it all comes back to you.

"Is that a sprain?" an innocent young man asked me in Aspen one crisp winter night as I hobbled gracelessly on the ice on my crutches.

"No, it's a sponge," I retorted, only to have the joke lost in his ignorance. How many people know that in the 1970s the newest development in prosthetics was in the "cosmesis" of the prosthesis, specifically, the endoskeletal modular, an artificial leg made of sculpted foam on the outside and a steel tubular skeleton inside.

"What's wrong with your leg, darlin'?" another brave and curious soul asked me in a Steamboat Springs bar one day last summer.

"Nothing…I hope," I responded dramatically. "This thing cost $2,400. Can't afford to break it."

"Oh, I'm so sorry," he prostrated himself before me and begged me to forgive him for thinking the least.

"Don't be sorry," my quick friend Laura admonished. "Buy us a round of drinks and you'll be even." Always directly proportionate to the amount of respect and compassion your friends have for you is the amount of quipping advantage they'll take of your traumatic personal loss.

Out on a limb, one foot in the grave, things are precarious enough that you shouldn't have to cup your ear every day, anticipating that inevitable questioning reminder, "What are you doing on crutches?"

"Motorcycle," I used to answer. This response, however true, proved unsatisfactory after a while as it usually invited further questioning of the gory details. "My [uncle, cousin, brother, best friend, old boyfriend — you fill in the blanks] was in a motorcycle accident once." Sure, I can relate, but rather than bring up the past, I like to be current.

"Feel my thigh," I offer in the pub when a suave, debonair young man wants to know what's wrong with my leg. If they dare do that, they usually have the fortitude to sit through a small discourse on Barroom Prosthetics, 101. And you know the guy has passed the course when you turn the other cheek, in my case hard plastic, and he doesn't knock you on the side of the head for breaking the tips of his fingers on your bionic bun.

You know you're with a real smooth guy when he says, "You do more for a prosthesis than some women do for a French bathing suit," as my friend Fred once said.

"Crustacean Curves," Fred calls me in reference to my "bucket socket," which is the plastic armadillo skin that wraps around my rib cage like a 19th-century corset and supports the weight of the fake leg that is attached on the left side. Sometimes when he's being particularly lecherous he calls me Lobster Lady — soft on the inside, hard on the outside — and threatens to crack me with the biggest pair of nutcrackers known to man and dip me in a 100-pound vat of butter. Now there's a guy with imagination.

"Cosmesis of the prosthesis" means that your artificial leg looks good, like a real leg. It's harder for a woman than a man, because of the curves, but most prosthetists won't even try to make it look good because they're men and they think it's frivolous. I'm lucky my leg man is radical: He thinks you can have cosmesis without sacrificing functionalism. The only drawback to this is when you almost wish the thing didn't look so real.

One day on the Trailways bus from Amherst to Boston I was seated next to a young man of the world, about 14 years old. What he lacked in physical stature he made up for in bravado.

"Oh yeah. I skip school all the time and ride the bus to Boston. I cruise the city and pick up new chicks."

"Well, that's great you're such an adventurer," I said, and we talked of adventure until I started to get sleepy and ended the conversation by putting my head back and shutting my eyes.

When I awoke, my seatmate was leaning back in ecstasy, mouth agape. I looked down to see him stroking my left thigh in such a slow, sensuous caress that it's a wonder the sponge didn't sizzle and melt. Of course I never felt a thing and was embarrassed. I hate to think what he thought he was doing for me. In retrospect, it would have been fun to offer to take it off so he could get better acquainted with the object of his affections.

You know your cosmesis is good when someone thinks it's real and the leg is not even on you. Like the year I was at the ski show in Boston.

It was a long night, with lots of walking. I longed to be a monoped. With 13 less pounds to drag around I could slip through the crowds easier. I took off my leg in the ladies' room, thinking, "She'll be okay in here." I sat her on the stool and locked the door of the stall, and after throwing a skirt on, I climbed out from underneath. My jeans were still on the leg. When I came back half an hour later, I was panicked. Could I be in the wrong bathroom? Carolimb was gone. I walked outside and was grabbed by a Hynes Auditorium security guard. "Excuse me Miss, did you lose a...ah, are you...ah...missing...ah..." He started out forcefully and was now faltering.

"Yes!" I responded frantically. "My prosthesis is gone! I'm looking for my leg. I left it in the ladies room and it's gone!"

It turned out a washroom matron had fainted when she saw my leg, stretched out, jeans and one shoe, lying on the stall floor. Apparently it had fallen off the stool. She thought it was a drug overdose.

So the security guard marched me to the head office, where the big show-business people from Ski Magazine, Ski Industries of America, and the ski show were hanging out. I played the scene to the hilt. I mean, I was mad. What right did they have bringing her in their office and undressing her? Hmpf.

"Carolimb! Caught with our pants down again," I exclaimed to my NOT better half. I picked her up, threw her over my shoulder, knee to foot hanging down my back like a ponytail, and — leaving the whole room wondering if this wasn't one of the handicapped skiers' booth consciousness-raising techniques — I bolted back to the ladies room, this time to reunite.

Nah, it's not all fun and games. Sometimes it's sad. Like when you have to get a new one, because your old model doesn't work anymore. You have to throw away that thing that was a part of you for so long, to which you had finally become accustomed.

Or, of course, you can make a planter out of it, pawn it, have it bronzed, and put on your parents' TV set. I suppose you could disassemble the ribcage bucket from the leg and use it for a creative trash receptacle, or have it mounted at your local taxidermist even.

Too bad you couldn't trade it in for parts. Keep it in your closet a few extra years and resell it in an antiques shop. Now that would make for a more profitable loss.

Circa 1976. Earlier this day, Karen Witt and I met photographer Phil Miller outside the Boston Public Library. We smiled hugely at him, recognizing another gimp. Seeing two lovely ladies sitting on a fountain, he smiled in return. "Is that a pylon you're wearing?" I asked him. He scowled and asked if it was so obvious. We both pulled up our pant legs, and I said, "We're

amputees, too!" He finally smiled back. He later offered to buy us both lunch if we would stay so he could take more pictures. We three became fast famous friends. When I left Boston for Winter Park, he gave me these pictures framed as a series.

1979, Paris. My bus pass in Paris took me all over the city for three weeks. It was even better than taking a tour bus.

C'est la Vie
(2001 *Have Crutch Will Travel*)

When my friend Louise was studying mime in Paris in 1979, I went to visit her. She explained in advance that I could stay with her, but we would only have time together on the weekends. She worked as a governess for a French family and was studying under Etienne Descroux, the great Marcel Marceau's teacher; she had a very busy schedule.

Louise had asked her English friends Patrick and Helen to hold an overnight welcome party. Patrick and Helen lived in the suburbs in a ground floor flat which accomodated my crutches quite nicely.

That first night outside Paris I stayed up late and read The Tao of Physics, while Louise tossed and turned with leg cramps from her exacting physical discipline, and with nausea--probably due to nerves getting us from the airport to the Arc de Triomphe in a small Peugeot with Blondie singing "One way or another, I'm gonna find ya, I'm gonna getcha, getcha, getcha," matching the whirling beat of traffic around the traffic circles.

That night I began stereotyping the French. The French, it seemed, ate so late, the food was so bland, the vegetables cooked until the colors bled out — or maybe the whole meal was leeks — I don't know, but the next morning I felt like the typically ugly American asking where we could have a Denver omelette with hot peppers for breakfast.

When I finally got to Louise's place — oh, mon dieu! She lived in a six-floor walk-up one-room apartment called a "chambre de bonne" (maid's room) on the Avenue Marceau. Her street was one of the spokes in the arrondissement of the Champs Elysees, not far from the Arc de Triomphe and the "bateaux mouches," or flyboats, on the opposite side of the Seine.

There was no elevator, the stairs were so steep you could eat dinner on the one above you, the room so tiny, I had to prop Carolimb up in the bidet. After a second night of floor sleep, Louise went off to work, and I headed out to get a "carte orange," a monthly bus pass, so I could ride around the city sightseeing first class from the windows of the autobus, without a tour guide, as it were.

The next day, I wore Carolimb down the stairs of Louise's building and figured that while Carolimb gave me a lap and a rear end good for sitting in the cafés, she would be a burden once I needed to walk. I looked for a place to stow her after I had my coffee in the Café Marceau, but I was not very successful. So, I dragged her around Paris, to the Tuilleries and the Eiffel Tower, where I considered creating a public sensation by throwing her off the monument. I settled for an éclair at another café, where I met Brenda, an Englishwoman whose husband's company had moved them from South Africa to Paris. Brenda was visiting Paris on her own, too. We compared notes and both agreed that only French women knew the right attitude with which to travel alone in Paris.

The problem was the men. Everywhere I went, if I was alone, I was followed by a strange — foreign of course, but usually Middle Eastern — man who would make a fool of himself if I acknowledged him with as much as a glance. I told her about the first "follower." I was trying to find a park in Paris that allowed people to lie on the Parisienne grass. They didn't mind dogs on the grass, but human beings would be scooped up by the local police if they stepped on a blade. I was followed from fenced park to fenced park by a man I had smiled at and said hi to.

Finally, at Pont Neuf (one of the bridges over the Île de Cité Park where the hippies and European traveling bums hung out), I saw people sitting on the grass. As I headed down the long cement steps and took my place on the green, my talking shadow sat down next to me. I politely answered questions until I asked him to leave so I could take a nap. He wouldn't leave, so I got angry. Naturally, he wanted to nap with me, thought I was beautiful when I was mad. Searching out a policeman at one of the boats on the river, I got up in frustration and prepared my speech for the policeman.

In French I asked him, "Could you help me? I have asked this man to leave me alone, but he keeps following me."

I was surprised when the gendarme seemed to understand my French, even more shocked when he responded in a Maurice Chevalier flourish of English. "Eef I wahr heem, I wohd follow yoh, too!"

Brenda and I laughed over that one, and we both began a practice of watching as French women shot their noses up in the air and brushed off every man who approached them. Brenda and I performed the past tense of the verb "rendezvous" nearly every day after that. We looked at tourist brochures and our bus passes and figured the routes to Place de Vosges, Centre du Pompidou, and the Louvre — and then we made a morning and afternoon of each.

Lots of stopping to rest at cafés, I was always looking for a bathroom in Paris. "Monsieur. Ou est les toilettes?" was my most practiced phrase next to "Si vous parlez lentment, je peux comprendre." If you speak slowly, I can understand. Invariably the answer to my question regarding the nearest lavatory was "La bas," which means "down there," or "over there." It seemed to always be said in such a gruff, low tone, I half expected people to say "up there" in a high-pitched voice.

The public restrooms, I learned, were almost always down steep cement steps into the sewer-like basements of centuries-old restaurants and cafes where you had to squat over a hole in the ground covered with a grate. Carolimb, my artificial leg, wasn't a squatting kind of a gal, so I had to take her off, disengaging my right leg from her pair of pants and, once we were separated, prop her up, etc. After the first day dragging the dead weight, I put Carolimb in the trash room on the first floor of Louise's building. I then walked up the stairs and didn't put her on again, except to have coffee at the Café Marceau in the morning. After coffee, I rechecked her into the trash room before going off for the day.

When I got back one afternoon, the concierge was standing in the lobby, certainly not waiting for an elevator. When she saw my crutches her eyes widened in frightful realization, no, I think relief.

"Cest votre jambe!" It's your leg!

"Oui," I said, in the off-handed breathless French manner of "whey."

"What happened?" She exclaimed in French.

"Motorcycle," I replied, pronouncing "cycle" (seekel) with an excellent French accent.

"Oh, non! C'est triste!" she gushed.

She looked to me for confirmation of her opinion on how sad it was, and I shrugged, "Non," I corrected her, "C'est la vie!" Then in French I said what I never had even said to myself, but it was just right, "le mot juste," at that moment.

"C'est ma vie!" I headed up the stairs aware I'd set the scene for how natural it was for my leg to be resting in the trash room. Carolimb, the steep stairs, the trash room, the English-speaking policeman, and the coffee and basement bathrooms. "That's life! That's my life!"

1979, Paris. Carolimb, on me wearing jeans as I pose by the Seine.

It's hard to spot me at the top of the stairs with my crutches in front of Montmartre, but I'm on the right.

Among the artists along the Seine.

Circa 1940. My mother, decades before kids and Filene's, passed on to her daughters her love of fashion.

Filene's Basement

(1985 revised 1995 for *Howlings*)

Pictures of my mother when she was young show a smiling girl with a voluptuous figure, stylishly dressed and proud of face, with her chin aimed toward the gods. The mother I knew was short, rounded-out and flattened down, not exactly stylish but still proud of face with her chin held high.

She seemed to shorten and widen with age, not just because she quit wearing heels but also because she was worn down with work.

At 50, her varicose veins and calloused hands hinted at her hard life. The grief of losing two children, raising six more alone, and tending to a husband with a mental illness was compounded when I, her eldest, lost my leg. She shared the pain of that injury and loss, becoming my champion for life. She taught me to survive, to thrive, and in the case of my favorite store in Boston, she taught me the skills of hunting and gathering in the women's world of fashion.

Born into the middle class, she didn't know poverty until she had children. She loved nice clothes but only shopped thrift and second-hand stores until her last child was old enough to go to school — and after my father was hospitalized. Once she finally could make enough money to buy things, she made up for nearly two decades of penury.

"Hello! Hell-lo-o-o!" She cheerfully bustled into the kitchen, opening its door with her foot or shoulder, her arms usually full of shopping bags, yelling her greeting, often with a giggle in her throat that dared you to smile back. I don't remember her ever dragging herself in sad and tired. She always entered a room with that salutation: "Hell-lo-o!" It has become an emblem to me, a creed, a contract made with the world that though pain and suffering abound, there will always be a smile and a happy greeting to counterbalance their weight.

"All the college girls were grabbing these," she'd say when she came home from a spree. My sisters and I looked at her suspiciously. "You mean they wear undershirts in college? And overalls? Are you sure? No one's wearing undershirts with little bows at the top in high school, Ma." After a while that line about college girls became a joke between us. "Those college girls will wear anything!" We came to trust her judgment, however, as we crowded around the peach-colored Filene's bags she pulled from her huge shopping sacks.

Under new ownership, Filene's Basement today is a mere shadow of its formerly famous bargain-hunting background. Back then — from the department store's *tres cher*, chic, and spacious first floor — descending the escalator to The Basement resembled moving through a tableau of the Dante's ebullient angels in Heaven to the toiling souls in Purgatory.

Nothing but my nimble-footedness helped me negotiate the escalators on crutches, but my mother's fine antennae often saved me from the coat hanger side-slip, since coat hangers carpeted the tile floors. In The Basement, pandemonium reigned; like bargain sharks in a feeding frenzy, shoppers made Filene's a test of survival of the fittest. Even Governor Michael Dukakis shopped for his suits there. With crutches at my sides I fended off the jostling crowds; ahead my mother blazed the trail.

Shoes, bras, bathing suits, men's ties, robes, belts, and sweaters were heaped into piles and burst out of wooden bins. The bins were set closer together than the gambling machines in Vegas, and from the moving stairs, they stretched as far as the eyes could see.

Every manner of person lost their manners in Filene's. Once I saw two women digging deep into a pile of shoes and pulling so hard each ended up with one shoe from a pair. Each registered horror at this outcome, but old King Solomon couldn't have settled the dispute. Reluctant to relinquish their finds, they resembled two birds bickering over the same worm.

Designer clothes, once ever so posh, were ghettoized in Filene's, lying on the floor, while others were homeless, waiting for someone to recognize their potential. My mother instructed me to inspect the merchandise: A missing button, a ripped seam, an irregular size, no problem. But if you had to spend $7 to have it cleaned before you wore it made the garment less worth buying. Filene's sales dictated our wardrobes: spring clothes in the summer and summer clothes in the fall. Still, in those days Filene's prices rewarded the diligent.

My mother knew my taste and the specific style I needed to offset the asymmetry of my figure, and when we entered Filene's Basement, we both hunted with a selective vengeance for the right combination of style, color and price.

"Oh, Carolyn, dear. It's you! It's beautiful. We have to get it," she would say in her throaty voice. She held the coat hanger under my chin, and against my chest a purple silk dress fell to shin length, making my leg look less lonely at hem line. We both looked up to consult Filene's Calendar of Automatic Markdowns: Two weeks in the basement, 20% off; three weeks 50%; four weeks 75%; and if an item lasted longer, you brought it to customer service, and they literally gave it to you. The excitement over finding an item over 75% can't be described unless you've caught a rainbow trout in a wading pool...with your bare hands.

"Okay, how much is it — $25?" I was ever so cool and rational when she was expressive. "Marked down from $115...okay. Hang on to it, but let's look for a few more." Then I looked closely at the tag. "You know, this will be marked down in two days — maybe we should wait."

We became more and more strategic in our approach. Sometimes if we didn't have the money, we'd stuff the dress behind a few racks and come back to get it the next day. We'd go from rack to rack yelling across to each other like partners in a goldmine, sifting new nuggets to the surface. She could see from my face if I grew tired and advised me about the row of seats she saw near the shoe section. "Why don't you sit down and rest, dear, and I'll bring you some dresses over." I'd drop into a chair wearily, thankfully.

One night, soon after I learned to ski, we read in the paper about a sale on ski clothes. What luck!

Half an hour before Filene's was to open, the store, which covers a full square city block, was surrounded by a mob of ready shoppers. When the clock hit nine, the women roared through the doors and poured down the stairs like a horde of grasshoppers. The clerks and salespeople must've caught their breath at the riotous flow.

My mother and I followed quickly on the heels of the crowd and were dismayed to see the racks literally swarmed by shoppers. As soon as an elevator opened and a rack was wheeled out, they lit onto it like locusts, forcing the clerks to give up the rack before it was even in place. "No wonder these clerks are always so loud and rude," my mother remarked, turning around to give the benefit of her raised voice to those who bore down heavily behind us.

"They must've got their training from crowds like this! Hmpf!"

But this day even Filene's clerks weren't ready for the onslaught. My mother had me sit against one of the two supporting posts around which the departments were laid out. My back to the dressing mirror, I watched the racks like a hawk. Each shopper collected on her arms as many items of clothing as her weight and bulk could bear and brought the lot to a square post, or a corner, to stake out her ground. A mirror had to be close by. I sighted two airline stewardesses taking their clothes off down to the underwear! I surveyed these encampments, and as soon as I saw a jacket, vest or ski pants tried on and discarded by a shopper, I signaled my mobilized mother, who would swoop down and ask, "Might we try that jacket on please since you're not going to buy it?" Some gave it up, others sat heavy on their roosts. After a while my mother and I had a nest of our own from which I remember I bought a yellow Head parka, blue warmups, and long underwear.

One year we actually caught a sale upstairs in Filenes' sports department. Later, when my mother and I sat down at a little salad bar table on the upper floor, we marveled at the deal. "And we didn't even have to fight a crowd! Can you imagine that!" These adventures were my mother's early lessons in transforming poverty into creative lifestyles. If you were willing to settle for fewer amenities, and if you were smart, you could look as good as rich people for one tenth the price. Fashion was a sort of compensation for poverty. I would later understand the ethic behind the welfare person's priorities: Pride in personal appearance offsets the ignominy of being poor. Having nice clothes is not a flagrant abuse of funds; it's a matter of buying some dignity at a very small price.

After capturing our bargains, we'd sit on the cement planters at the corner of Washington and Franklin streets near Woolworths, waiting for the bus. There we would be serenaded by urban troubadours, hats upside down on the pavement in front of them, performing for a penny or a dollar or two.

If we'd spent our last dime, we just tapped our toes and smiled a thanks to the musician, whether it was a gray-bearded saxophone player, a collegiate-dressed soprano, or a man with no legs on a skateboard, playing the accordion. We even smiled to the blind man who played the organ while his dog looked intelligently out at the crowd as though assessing their appreciation.

I can see my mother now, proud of face, her chin into the sun, smiling out at individual faces in the crowd, her shopping bags bouncing against her tapping toes, happy to live in the city of Boston with its accessible public transportation and its support for the arts. "To think you can be entertained while waiting for the bus! Isn't life grand?!"

1977. Posing with my mother before saying goodbye the day I moved to Colorado.

1981, Winter Park. Swinging wide for a gate; not the best form but I sure am having fun. Photo by ski team photographer Ray Bliese. They say it's never too late to have a happy childhood. I had my second chance in Winter Park.

Après Ski

(1996 *Howlings*)

I never thought I'd have to lose a leg to become athletic. That's how it happened, though, after my new friend Jane, a recent amputee herself, asked me if I'd like to go skiing.

"*What? And break my one and only leg?*" What is she, a masochist? I wondered. That was before I learned masochism is a prerequisite for being an athlete.

"Cale, most people break a leg because they cross their tips. We can't do that." I forgave her good attitude; however, I saw I had to be more sophisticated in my excuses.

"Skiing is an elitist sport," I sniffed. "You have to have money."

"It's free if you're disabled," she volleyed.

"But I don't know how," I said like the stubborn coward I was.

"They teach you," she offered to encourage me.

"Where are we supposed to get the equipment?" I didn't really want an answer.

"They loan it! Free," she added, and we recognized we'd both been through a major life crisis — and she had all the right responses to both of our excuses.

After the success of gracefully mastering crutches, I was soon to be humiliated by both the laws of physics and the athletic challenge of learning to ski with a body that was still a stranger to me.

Inside her car, parked outside the lodge, my new friend and I sat for several hours telling our stories. I told her, "When I was in high school I was a 'hoodsie.' The most athletic thing I ever did was run — and that was from the cops." I didn't mention I had been a bowler, since I only did it to wear the shoes and be ogled by the boys. She was a swimmer, played tennis and lacrosse in P. E. class. She too had never skied before.

When we entered the lodge, I felt like Ann Boleyn heading for my beheading. Then I saw a gathering of guys lounging at the fireplace drinking Schnapps and hot chocolate. Social life, now that I could relate to. Jane, who'd been entrusted with the directions, steered us both to the handicap skier station, where we stood on platforms and sat on benches. By the time I got all my gear, I was exhausted. "Okay. Let's hit the bar," I said cheerily. Instead we were led by our instructors into the frigid air to the hilltop. Unlike most ski resorts, at Haystack in Vermont you ski from top to bottom before taking your first lift back to the hilltop. Waiting at the top, our teacher, Fran, an imposing figure and 30-something three-tracker, instructed us on how to put on our skis and take up our outriggers.

Outriggers are crutch-like ski poles with 12-inch ski tips at the bottoms that ride over the snow, making a platform of three skis instead of two, thus the expression three-tracker. Once you become a really good skier like Fran, you ski with your one leg and use the outriggers to balance every once in a while. That first day, though, three skis weren't enough.

In the two years I had been an amputee, I had never worn pants. My vanity required long dresses that flared at the waist so I could also hide my loss of a hip. In these ski pants with the left pant leg tucked into the left side, I felt like a dorky stork standing over the ski as I readied to put my foot into the binding. My balance was good, but it did call for the earth to stand still.

With my crutches gingerly gripping the snow, I leaned down. The ski flew backward, and I flew forward. Fran caught me right in time and kept me from falling flat on my face. She held me around the waist while I got the ski on. I stood like a perturbed flamingo while Fran handed me the outriggers. Then the principles of friction vs. sliding demonstrated themselves. The first thing I did was treat the outrigger like a crutch and put some weight on it. Like a banana peel it slid out from beneath me. I was on my butt before my ski had even moved. I was stunned. Fran didn't offer to help me up. I hardly had strength to lift myself, let alone the fool outrigger at the same time.

Oh, my. I was most unhappy, and the cheerfulness around me made my mood more foul. My friend was already several hundred feet down the hill, a natural kinesthetic learner. "You can do it, Cale," someone gushed. Right. Each time I tried to get up, the ski slipped downhill, with me laying on its tail.

"Lay your ski across the fall line," yelled Fran. The fall line she had explained earlier was the path a ball would take if dropped down the hill. Fran sideslipped down to me, stopped my slide, and then lifted my ski — with my leg attached — up into the air, turned me around on my back and headed my ski across the slope. "You want to get up with your ski across the fall line and use the uphill outrigger to push up off the ground," she said.

"No, I don't. I want to go in and have some hot chocolate now," I grumbled to myself. My crutches, however, were 10 feet above me, my ski having slipped that far down the hill as I was trying to get up. I knew "Admiral Fran" — I now thought of her as the Admiral Von Trapp — would never bring them down to me. I was in for the duration. Her duration.

The day was a nightmare. My ski pants kept falling off me, and I couldn't pull them up without letting go of the outrigger and falling down myself. Those moments when I would get set upright, point downhill and start to get some speed, I'd instinctively lean back to keep the ski from going further down hill. Boom. Skiing taught me another law of physics: if you lean back, the ski goes forward faster; if you don't keep your weight centered, you're down.

"Bend your knee," she instructed, and I looked down to see what part of my body my knee might be.

The concept of turning was never introduced that day because I used up a flotilla of instructors trying to teach me to merely stay up. I could hear voices from uphill calling, "Kyle. Get UP!" and I thought, I'm glad I'm not this Kyle guy because I gotta sit down and rest. When I realized they were actually yelling at me, I was genuinely puzzled. Why rush to get up if I'm just going to fall down again?

When I finally got to the bottom of the hill, I collapsed in relief and created a snow angel. I didn't care if I embarrassed the other gimps. When I looked up into the blue sky, I saw a circle of trees, and realized I wasn't even cold. I was exhilarated. I looked uphill to see how far I'd come, and I felt a bolt of happiness. It wasn't that hard — as long as I didn't have to do it again real soon!

However, I was subsequently introduced to the converse of Newton's Law of Gravity: What goes down must come up again. At Haystack you skied down and took a T-bar up. A T-bar is a rope tow with an iron piece shaped like an upside down "T." A skier holds onto the stem with one hand, tucking one side of the "T" under her rear end, and is towed to the top.

This assumes that you have not only balance and strength in your leg, but a butt. No one made the connection that my pants were falling off because, not only had I lost a leg, but more than half my derrière. So no one could figure out why I was such a terrible spaz on the T-bar. It took the rest of the day to get me up it. Eventually one of the instructors skied me between his legs, his butt on the T, and my back leaning against him. If I get to the top, I asked him, can I stay there? He offered to buy me that hot chocolate himself. My hero!

The thing that was most exciting about that first day of skiing was that it ended. I came a few times more that winter, even conquering the T-bar, and by my last lesson I could traverse the slope and stay on my skis. The next year I discovered paradise at Sunapee, New Hampshire, where they had a chair lift. It would take at least one more season before I was strong enough to stand up from a sitting position, balance my body over the center of the ski, and turn with enough finesse to completely control my speed.

In five years I would be competing regionally and nationally, and in 1979 become the Women's National Three-Track Champion. In 1980 I represented my country in Olympic Games for Disabled in Norway. All that for a hot chocolate après ski?

All that because skiing gave my body back to me.

1977, Aspen. My first Rocky Mountain Regional races introduced me to many of the people with disabilities (blind and amps here) who would become part of the future U.S. and Canadian teams. I am with Canadian Champ Greg Oswald and world-class skier Danny Pufpaff, respectively. Photo by Didi Gough, who later became ski team break photographer.

1981, Press Cup at Winter Park. It was a special honor to represent the Winter Park Manifest with other Colorado newspapers, including the Post and the News. I was the only disabled skier in the group.

David, Jane and I pose with NEHSA while we were in Alpine Meadows, California.

Gimps on the Go
(2002 *Have Crutch Will Travel*)

When I was a kid I dreamed of becoming a foreign correspondent. It wasn't until my second road trip that I actually wanted to write about the experiences, exotic locations, and unique cultures I visited while traveling on crutches.

After my first road trip with my brother I was lucky enough to take a trip across the country with friends. We were three weekend skiers who had met on the ski slopes and whooped it up on the dance floor every chance we could. I had just graduated from college, David from high school, and Jane took a semester off her senior year for a road trip to the Handicap National Championships at Alpine Meadows in California. We were the dynamic trio: I was an affable amateur comedienne/fool; Jane, a passionate, political, and intellectual wit; and David, a tall, GQ (Gentleman's Quarterly), handsome 18-year-old equestrian who laughed in delight at our every uttering and who egged us both on with his appreciation.

Road trips are a special kind of travel; they are a running conversation between the car, its occupants, and the scenery. Like a melody box whose wheels wind up a road show of scenery, the images create their own rhythm: straight-ahead-asphalt, syncopated white lines and yellow, and trees to the side, always rushing, deciduous and evergreen. The hills and dales, hillocks and vales, haystacks and tumbleweeds, chipmunks and squirrels; dead cats and dead skunks "in the middle of the road." Dead ahead, the other casualties of the road are like static: dead bugs against the windshield — flies, bees, mosquitoes, butterflies — have to be tuned out or washed away.

The weather provides whimsical background arrangements: whether hot sun beating down, or happy little raindrops splattering, or pelting rain splats battering, it creates symphonies that in the colder climes might soften with snowflakes so light your windshield wipers screech or howl with snowstorms so ferocious you have to pull over to the side and wait. These melodies resound between the flat, broad runs through valleys and the steep, winding, hairpin-turning mountain passes over the peaks.

Playing amidst the wonderful tunes of the tape deck, the vibrations of car wheels on asphalt accompanied the sounds of silence: crunching granola, rustling bags as we reached for a drink or consulted the map. Jane and David spoke little, listening to the music, Cat Stevens' "Moonshadows," Linda Ronstadt's "Heart Like a Wheel," Frank Zappa and his Eskimo song, "Nanook, No, No. Don't go where the huskies go, and don't you eat the yellow snow."

Inside the car, I recognized the road trip melody box of passing scenery even when I wasn't watching it, and it got my mind to turning, storing up energy for that jack-in-the-box time when — Pop! — I'd interrupt the rhythm to give the commentary I'd stored up during all those miles of reading, reflection, and silent conversation with myself about this idea for a story called "Gimps on the Go," chronicling the adventures of myself and two amputee friends.

Every pit stop, we would make history as a public sensation, I mused.

In truth, before we had even made it past the hills of western Massachusetts, we were causing the public phenomenon I coined "gimp gawking." Jane, who's an above-knee amputee, walked pretty well. David's stump was longer, but he had a unique gait because of the new leg he had recently convinced a prosthetist to make — a peg leg. Like Jane he wore a socket over his stump, but instead of a hinging knee joint attached to the socket so the lower leg could swing through, the prosthetist created a recessed internal threading that allowed a straight piece of wood with counter threads at the top to screw into it.

So while Jane slightly limped, stiff-legged David thumped like Captain Ahab. When you add me to the mix, one leg on crutches, we were a funny-looking trio. While we were in the car, of course, I didn't wear my new bulky artificial leg; so when we made it to a truck stop or a local diner, the public met the fake leg, the peg, and the one-legged woman on crutches. And they stared. Some even spoke up.

"Are you a family?" one waitress asked. Said another at the same truck stop, "Now, were y'all in the same accident?" While David giggled, I usually cracked some wise aleck remarks like, "Yeah. We parked across the street and were hit by the same truck on our way in here." Jane was forced to play it straight and inform the person we were three amputee skiers on our way to Colorado. But she always had some funny remark to add, reflecting the irony of us being grouped as an accident when our trip was very deliberate, which brought an eruption of laughter from everyone involved.

"What's it like to travel with these two?" a truck driver asked David.

"They're not just gorgeous and intelligent," David said over his shoulder getting back in the car, "they're both crazy, too!"

The truck driver nodded as if to say "That's what I thought."

"I'm going to call it gimp-gawking," I told the front seat after we talked about this public sensation business.

Jane and Dave traded off the driver's seat of Jane's Saab; I was in a comfortable combination of horizontal reading and jack-in-the-box reporting and commentary from my position in the back seat. I might have been luggage, I was so small and compact with half a side gone — a portable passenger turned messenger each time I popped up with excitement and the need to speak. When we pulled close to a AAA trip-tik point of interest, I would sit up from my collapsed position and give the front seat the scoop. Somewhat serendipitously I acquired a coverless paperback book about ski bumming across America, which was, according to the book, a dying lifestyle.

"Listen to this! Not too far from Alpine Meadows is the magnificent Heavenly Valley Resort. Let's go there, too!"

"Yeah. But don't forget the California skiers said lodging is free at the Donner Spitz Inn," David said, "and you can stay past the nationals."

"I remember reading a postcard you sent to your friend Kate at the first nationals, David. You wrote: 'This place is swarming with amputees.' That cracked me up!" I'd never thought how he might refer to Jane and me, but I didn't much like the word amputees; it reminded me of doctors.

David had a delighted laugh that contrasted with his sometimes dry delivery. "How could I forget them? I can't imagine what it's going to be like staying at the top of Donner Pass with all those amputees under the same roof. At least we had different hotels in Winter Park."

"Not everyone is staying there, just the ones who want to," Jane said. "Do you remember at the last Nationals, these guys taking off their legs in the bar and drinking beer out of them?"

"I don't know how they could do that!" David said.

"Practice. It wasn't their first Nationals," I added. And we all laughed.

To put it mildly, the Nationals were a place where anything goes. Dozens of artificial legs lay discarded at the bottom of the ski lift during the day, and a party could start anywhere, anytime. While discovering the character of the quieter people was a joy for a chair lift ride, the disco dancing brought out the wild sides of those who couldn't express themselves on the slopes. The disco was a social opportunity not to be missed, even if you just watched.

"I remember thinking that these people loved life more than anything because they knew how close they had come to losing it. Especially the vets who lost friends in Vietnam. I hated the word 'gimp' before I went to the nationals," I said.

"I remember how conscious we were of our amputations before then," Dave said reflectively. Dave had lost his leg to cancer, and the silence around why he lost the leg and the fact that he went into the hospital one day with two legs and came out with one was confusing to a boy of 14. He found people's inability to talk about "The Big C" was insufferable, so meeting two articulate women near his age who were willing to talk freely about lots of things, including cancer and amputations, was liberating.

Jane and I were both freshmen in Amherst when we lost our legs on the same road eight months apart. Jane was in a van whose driver, deliberately trying to scare his passengers, accidentally crashed on Route 116 going south. I had been traveling north. We both came from large Irish families with tragic fathers and strong mothers. We were soul sisters; Dave was our little brother.

"We met so many new people, but we didn't have the freedom," Jane said, referring to our group-sponsored and -chaperoned trip. "I remember thinking how much fun we were going to have when we had our own wheels."

"Yeah, we couldn't have picked a better year for a road trip!" I said, leaning forward with excitement. In April, Canada was hosting the Canadian International Games for Disabled in Banff, Alberta.

"I'm just hoping we have enough money to make it to Canada. That's in two months." Jane said.

"Don't worry. We have connections," I reminded her, and we flew past a few more tumbleweeds before turning the tape deck back on.

I didn't know it at the time, but we were forging our identities and attitudes as amputees during this long trip. The insular joking of small groups is contagious, and we were becoming comfortable calling ourselves gimps. By the end of the trip I had developed — for the story I never wrote until 2000 — a whole vocabulary of gimpolalia: gimp gawking, gimp talking, and even gimp squawking. David and Jane likewise made up their own gimp lyrics to songs and created new expressions, but I coined gimp stalking. It applied both to "devotees," men who sought out amputee women simply because of their amputation, and to ourselves, when we related to someone and pursued them for the same reason, though with different intent. We were like evangelical Christians meeting, greeting, testifying, and, within hours, inviting people to share the story of how they lost their legs.

I remember one time in Wyoming picking up a hitchhiker, pant leg flapping in the breeze; when he got in he told us his car had broken down. We offered to take him where he wanted to go, and then asked him if he wanted to get something to eat. We usually bought food at grocery stores, but we splurged, eating out at a Denny's, learning more about him.

"You live here and you haven't been skiing?" we asked. "What do you do for fun?"

"Oh, I guess I'm just staying alive. Back from 'Nam. I do like to go riding around in my Corvette, smoking weed, and listening to a little music," he said with one of those 'can you dig it?' nods.

We couldn't. "Man, you have to get out there, meet some people, and get high on the mountains!" We three were interrupting each others' ideas on where he could ski, how he could get there, explaining how easy it was. "You just gotta stand up. Gravity does the work!"

By the time we gimp zealots reached Canada, the apex of our trip, we were designing a gimp logo with other amputees at the ski meet, working on an emblem for a tee-shirt. It was a variation of the '70s beach blanket graphic — a suggestive set of footprints, one set above the other, two lovers facing each other. Ours showed one footprint facing two feet and read "Gimps on Top." It debuted as unofficial memorabilia of the Canadian event. But I'm getting ahead of myself.

When we reached Colorado, we looked up our first connections in Boulder who took us to ski Lake Eldora, which was open even at night. How exotic! At Winter Park we met someone who knew how to get a free ski pass at Vail and Loveland. What a blast! In all kinds of weather we were out there wearing ourselves out and loving it. Everywhere we went, we met one or two new handicap skiers. What a small world Colorado skiing was! In Aspen we looked up a friend of David's who gave us a place to stay and week-long tickets to ski Snowmass, which was the single greatest contribution to our improving ski technique.

In the mountains of Colorado, breathing in, it's a special kind of breath you take above 10,000 feet, filled with sky and clouds and snow and converging lines and planes and notches. It's all so beautiful, the infinite colors and variety of cloud shapes, the pure snow and its blue shadows, the lines and planes and curves of brown earth providing clues to old railroad tracks and hiking trails in summertime. I didn't want to take my eyes off the view. It was at once stunning yet terrifying. The idea of getting to the bottom was daunting. Warrior-like aggression summoned, I broke the trance of viewing the tableau and became part of it.

When you are so totally in motion and your eyes are filled with nature's terrible grandeur, things fall away. My mind took in new thoughts. When these Colorado mountains were first created, nature had wrought violence upon the earth. Yet it's so peaceful now. These huge upheavals of earth were created by glaciers that cut across land mass, and now I'm cutting across with my ski. I may have one foot in the grave, but my other foot is still touching earth. I was still part of it, but I wasn't still; I was carving a path, picking a line through the best snow in the world.

It differed from skiing back East, where the trees are all bare-brown, the hills are round, and the conditions are hard-packed to boilerplate. I remember breathing in at the top of the chair lift in New England — where the paths seemed few, knowing how many times I'd fall down, that other people would see me down and vulnerable like that, and it would be so damn hard to pick up my body and start again. I could feel my asthma wheeze kick into my breath. It was so cold, so harsh — what about this is fun? I'd wonder. Where can we stop and have some food? Then there would be that point when, inevitably, because of the adrenaline it was fun. But it was never fun for long because I tired easily.

While we were skiing down those trails in Snowmass day after day, we were building our ski lungs and legs, breathing in constantly, being called to breathe in new life with each new effort, to exchange molecules and energy with the same atmosphere in which the mountains abide. One minute we were skiing, then, like birds of play, we were flying, held aloft, floating down the scene of mountains and trees and clouds and skis, and at the bottom we were on our knees, exhausted and praying for sleep. We skied every day we could, and every day, we could see that we were getting better. It was hard to leave Aspen, but we needed to move on. So, we called our Utah connections — Sally, an amputee in her 30s, and her self-proclaimed "pet normie" husband Ralph (call-me-Steve) Peterson.

It didn't seem there could be anything better than Colorado snow, but Snowbird ski resort was a revelation. There we took our first tram ride. Though the trails seemed more difficult, the light snow and the wide-open Wasatch mountain range scenery enchanted us. Several days at Snowbird created a high as difficult to describe as manna from heaven is hard to imagine; the snow was so good you could eat it. Like bread rising, my chest rose with every inhalation, and I was filled with energy, new oxygen for the cells. I felt great satisfaction and a kind of spirituality. Skiing Utah was like a breathe-and-feel-good body vibration that made you smile and talk to strangers.

It was warm enough at the Petersons in Roy, Utah, to sunbathe and clean the car. Steve helped us with our roof rack, gave us new skis, and spiffed up our outriggers with decals and flags. We met a whole new contingent of handicap skiers in Utah for whom Jane, David, and I were a complete novelty with our Boston accents, gimpolalia and our outrageous stories, which we were always expanding. Sally had found friends for life and didn't want us to leave. We stayed for weeks with the Petersons.

We headed off to California, where the color and pageantry of the nationals contrasted with the funkiness of the old barn that had once housed snow blowers and the men who operated them overnight on Donner Pass. Doug Pringle had purchased the old barn and turned it into a ski lodge called the Donner Spitz Inn. We all traded stories of how hard the wind blew through the cracks in our walls and against the ceilings of our dorm the night before. Legion were tales of alleged cannibals, the eponymous Donner Party, which started out so late in the year in 1846 that they got stranded over the winter by a snowstorm and resorted to eating one another to stay alive. At our dinner table each evening, everyone delighted in controversies, like when a BK (below-the-knee amputee) fell at the last gate and his fake leg fell off: Should officials mark him DNF (did not finish), or should he be able to keep the race time his leg turned in?

Most endearing were the on-the-road characters who, like us, were taking road trips. We met Larry the Irish Eskimo, another veteran, who would remark he needed to lie down and "check my eyelids for pinholes." Wild Bill was a tall BK who wore suede lederhosen over his leg, which he decorated colorfully.

The 6-foot-tall veteran was 19 and a helicopter pilot when he lost his leg below the knee in Vietnam. He was called Wild Bill, not just for his appearance and distint skiing style, but for his generally unconventional personality. Lifting his arms wide then dropping them, he swooped like an eagle when he came into a turn. He told me he spoke Russian, and I believed him, as it fit with his aesthetic sensibilities. He was a lover of classical music and played his favorite music for race day on an innovative audio headset of his own design. Wired into an 8-track tape-deck pack on his back and bulky earphones, he took off out of the start gates, listening, he told me, to "The William Tell 1812 Overture." While I watched him fly down the course, in my mind's ear I could hear the fireworks version played by the Boston Pops Orchestra on the Fourth of July, the one with the real cannons firing. One year several of us on the chair lift watched him miss a gate in a downhill event during a white-out; he sailed, gracefully as a bird, over a building-size boulder at trail's edge and landed unhurt. However, they did cancel the downhill that year.

Constant was the sound of hairdryers as different people patched with fiberglass their plastic prostheses broken by a good day of skiing. Everyone admired Al Hayes, a double AK (above-the-knee amputee) Vietnam Vet and a handsome New York rehab physiatrist. Although shorter legs yielded a lower center of gravity and control, Al chose to tower and wobble rather than give up his former six-foot height for a shorter pair of legs. He even wore Cuban heels. What a guy!

In California our trip became long and strange. We ran out of money, had nothing left from our food stores but potato chips and Ragu for dipping. We got lost looking for a legendary rehab hospital, Rancho Los Amigos.

We became depressed and had to have money wired. We had met people at the Nationals with whom we then drove to San Francisco, staying with some motorcycle enthusiasts and making tapes for our further travels. We needed to spend enough time there so that we could end up in Canada in April. But soon we were itching to ski, so we called the Petersons — again.

"You crazy gimps are invited to attend the U.S. Ski Team fundraiser," Steve told us over the phone. "We'll have your credentials waiting for you in Park City." Out came the map, and we doubled back to Utah to attend the Jill St. John Paul Masson Celebrity Ski Meet. I remember feeling like we had arrived in the Emerald City, the merry old Land of Oz, and free food for the whole week. We who'd slept in cars and trailers and eaten chips for dinner were now put up in posh Park City condos with pools, Jacuzzis, saunas, and a liter of Paul Masson wine on each of our beds. The final night is still part of my dreams.

Lowell Thomas was the keynote speaker. I remember him quipping that older people weren't forgetful, they just had more to remember; it was a twist on things that appealed to me. Kind of like Hal O'Leary's point that all skiers are handicapped by the size of their feet, so we use skis to lengthen them, outriggers to stabilize.

We joined the Utah gimps who represented the handicap skier community at tables with the U.S. Ski Team. I watched the U.S. skier Andy Mills flirt with one of the stars of the hit movie *Nashville*, the newly famous country singer Ronnie Blakely, whom we had listened to in the car on tape; Jane, David and I sang along with her, "American Beauty. You've got me blushing like a rose." After Lowell Thomas spoke, and we all ate our surf-n-turf, they cleared out the chairs, and the party rolled onto the wood floors of what must have been a big ballroom.

I remember feeling as naturally high as the chandeliers, dancing on one leg as smoothly as if I had two. I moved around in my mind in what seems now impossible ways, dreaming Ginger/Astaire. Looking back like this I wonder if I was as smooth as I imagined, but I felt so proud of my balance and strength, my skiing groove was blending with my accomplished dance style. I was tired of watching other people party and flirt. "I am not a spectator," I remember thinking. Around the same time I had a grandiose exchange with Ronnie Blakely, who was one of the few other people left at the end of the night. David spoke to her first when the five of us were at a table watching the few other people dance. "I just wanted to tell you," he said. "We love your album 'American Beauty.' We've been listening to it nonstop on our way cross country."

She was a star-studded beauty, for sure, and she gushed with a southern accent. "Everybody's been so great," she said. "Everyone's been complimenting me. You have no idea what it feels like to have so many admirers!"

"Oh, but we do," I said, disabusing her of her misperception of us.

At that point in April, Utah skiing became more like water skiing at the lower-elevation ski areas. We needed to go north, so we went to Jackson Hole to visit Charlene Rawls, our Wyoming connection.

We were running on frayed nerves because Jane and David had driven all day, and I had my usual phantom pain attack from sitting too long, but we didn't want to spend our money on lodging. We tried to contact Charlene, who had told us to go to any bar and ask for her.

Hundreds of antlers piled in one spot in the town square gave us a clue where to find the Cowboy Bar, where all the barstools were horse saddles. We had no money to buy a beer at the Cowboy Bar, but we did get treated to a few shots called kamikazes. Every waitress or waiter in town seemed to be a friend of Charlene's, who'd lost her leg below the knee and was quite the downhill racer, but few knew where she lived. We stayed in a hotel the first night out of desperation. The next night I slept in the car in 20 below zero cold because I was allergic to the cat in Charlene Rawls' teeny tiny mobile home just outside the Jackson Hole resort.

At the last edge of its grid, the town of Jackson Hole even had a little ski area, the Snow King. At the Snow King Resort, we were invited to ski for free by the manager who was also a gimp, due to polio. I remember feeling so competent I chose to ski over a jumping bump, wiped out on my outriggers; a black and blue on my left breast developed into a healthy rainbow of colors that lasted over the rest of the trip to remind me I wasn't that good a skier yet. In Jackson we could feel the excitement of the cowboy who had ridden long and hard and found a rest stop, a watering hole. Even though we couldn't afford a place to stay, the gorgeous Tetons, the Snake River, the galloping beat of country western rhythm and blues played on electric guitar roused our spirits.

But neither the five fabulous days in Utah nor our reprieve in Jackson Hole was anything compared to our last stop on the amputee ski bum line: Alberta, Canada (Note:

Actual date for Celebrity Ski Meet in Park City, Utah was *after* Canadian International Ski Meet in Banff, Alberta, Canada).

The Canadian International Games were hosted by the Canadian government, Sunshine Village Ski Resort, and the Banff Springs Hotel. A room at the hotel cost a handicap skier only $10 a night, we were told, and we had budgeted for it.

As we drove through the resort town with its boardwalks and shops, asking directions to the Banff Springs Hotel, none of us knew what to expect. As we approached, the hotel seemed to rise like a castle through the mists. Hewn of granite from the surrounding mountains, it was topped with turrets and cupolas above balconies of many different sizes and shapes. A river appeared to be winding through it. The snow on the trees reminded me of an embroidered tapestry.

Inside were large function rooms, rooms of state, halls where each night a different event was planned to welcome all countries to share information in symposia aimed at understanding not only disability but different cultures. Skiers from France, Germany, and England joined the North Americans, and there was a Japanese delegation. The different exhibits hinted at a disability culture so varied that any able-bodied visitor would be enriched by the vision of what individuals with disabilities had always seen for themselves: life on the go, with unique problems, rife with creative solutions, visions, and technologies. To a young mind it was a vision of hope and a society of inclusion. I felt inspired to be an ambassador, learning to say hello in different languages and resorting to pantomime when the person encountered assumed I could converse beyond that.

At the formal occasions, we greeted old friends and met new ones. Many of the U.S. veterans came, although in Banff, the toll taken by the Vietnam War wasn't apparent; the young men our age were amputees from disease or injury. Before one of the parties, Wild Bill sought out Jane and me to sew on a button for him. He looked like he was of another age, wearing a ruffled white Edwardian shirt with a velvet suit and knee-length britches, a velvet-flowered cover for his plastic leg.

Mornings, we drove a winding road along brooks, streams, rivers — mountain goats staring serenely from rock ledges — to the bottom of the mountain resort, Sunshine Village. There, the activity wasn't about competition as much as recreation, exchange, and education. Thus I found myself on the hill one morning in a clinic where for more than an hour we were initiated into the mystery of the sport. How many times had I heard, "It's all in the knee"? This teacher had another angle.

"It's all in the ski." They taught us how to control our ski with our ankle and boot. I hadn't taken a ski lesson since we left New England. "Feel your shins at the front of your boot. Feel your ankle, how if you roll the ankle into the hill you can feel the edge of your ski bite into the snow; now roll your ankle in the other direction." What sacred words did he use, what incantation isolated my ankle and animated my ski into the direction of the hill? It was trance-like. I was ready, and I got it. I was learning to ski my ski because I was suddenly strong enough and confident enough in my body to pay attention. I rejoiced in this knowledge, and promised myself to always stay physically strong and healthy.

In the afternoons we socialized at a warming house after skiing. I discovered how much more easily you could stand in one place and pivot with your ski boot on, and Jane and I were dancing like that hooting and hollering. "Whoo-hoo-hoo," I said to get David to join us. It worked, so I gave my banshee cry to all the monoped wallflowers, daring them to join us.

I remember one day taking a lift up to a half-glacier mountaintop. The Canadian Matterhorn was at eye level; I was feeling on top of the world. I was at tundra level, mountaintops like church spires surrounding me. No one I knew was anywhere around. A deep revelation came to me, a feeling of awe and gratitude I had never felt before. The feeling was reverent and eternal. I would never have been here, known this moment of bliss, this world of good people if I hadn't gone through the hell of my accident and its aftermath.

Suddenly I knew I was going to be all right. I was going to have a good life. Life is good. Thank you, God. Thanks for my life. With wings on my arms, my ski under me working with my spirit, I steered my foot toward the glade of trees below and, whooping and hollering, I sang and praised God. For the first time, I chose to take not the fastest route but the long meandering way down, skiing between the trees toward the bottom.

There I exchanged outriggers for crutches and hurried to join everyone at the warming house. One of the Japanese skiers was walking toward me, and I racked my brain for the right greeting. Was it "Conichiwa"? Or was it "Ohio?" Not sure, but smiling at him anyway, I was surprised when he greeted me first.

"Whoo-hoo-hoo!" he hollered. As he ran past me I doubled over in laughter recognizing my banshee cry.

When we returned from Banff, our melody box stopped at the Massachusetts state line, where we popped a bottle of champagne and toasted our safe return and the newly bonded gimp friendship we had formed.

The next year I returned to Banff, this time with my boyfriend Scott. The first day when we entered the elevator at the Banff Springs I was pleased to see there was again a Japanese contingent. Several Japanese people in the elevator seemed to recognize me, and I was puzzled when one turned to me and said, "Ah, Cale san. Number-one Japanese movie star." I laughed, and when two of the people got off the elevator, another turned to me and said, "Did you know that was the Prince of Japan who addressed you?"

The mystery was solved two evenings later when the Japanese premiered their movie of 1976, and there was David on celluloid showing the Japanese how he took off his peg and screwed it back on again. There Jane and I were on the dance floor. And in many other places, there was I, Cale-san Number One Japanese movie star, whooping and hollering and generally hamming it up, having the time of my life.

Top: 1976, Gimps on Top crowd, Jane, Greg, David, Cale, friend, Irish Eskimo Larry, Madeline.
Top right: Banff Springs Hotel, Alberta, Canada.
Bottom right: 1976, Sunshine Village. The spot where I had my peak experience on the slopes.

1983, Squaw Valley, California. Handicap Nationals Giant Slalom. The Comeback Kid.

Paradise Regained

(1996 Howlings)

For five years I lived in the mountains, a dream for many writers, certainly for every skier a life of bliss. From 1977 to 1983, when people said to me, "Oh, you're on an extended holiday," they meant: "You're a lousy ski bum on vacation." The truth was that each day I lived in Winter Park, Colorado, was a Holy Day, a sacred event God offered me at rising.

When one loses a leg, as I did at 19, the ease and grace of walking are lost. Skiing on one leg is like flying in the clouds. Earth to paradise, paradise to earth. I tried to spend as much time as I could skiing in the clouds.

I can recall certain mornings sitting on the chair lift, which were epiphanies as the silence opened up my senses to the moment. A zephyr wind when it rustled the evergreens mottled the cerulean blue sky, sugaring snow off branches. The sunlight, sifting through the crystalline chambers, sparkled flakes like fairy dust in a disappearing puff. After a momentary paperweight snowstorm, the silent stillness resumed, broken only by the groan of one of the old chair lifts.

Riding higher and higher up the slopes toward the mountain's top, I picked a path below. When the lift deposited me, I glided smoothly onto the trail over which I had just soared.

The mountain beckoned. Shadows of the treetops wing-tipped the sides of the path, creating a wider road of blue-white powder that called out to be traveled. Follow the Blue Powder Road. I was Dorothy winding my way to Oz through fields of poppies, only I didn't fall asleep. I came alive in every fiber of my being as I used each muscle in my body to wind up and down through hills and troughs of gentle moguls.

The children of skiing's rhythm method, "moguls" are bumps in the snow that make you turn. Each skier who banks a turn through powdery snow helps carve a rhythm as the pile-up of soft substance creates the mounds against which the next skier will bank or ski over the top. The steeper the hill, the deeper the moguls. Ski instructors warn their under-six-year-old students to "watch out for mogul mice."

The only evil that lurked in my paradise was the green-eyed monster of jealousy I encountered in acquaintances and sometimes friends envious of my unabashed choice of heaven over purgatory.

"She lives in a postcard." "What's she doing out there, anyway? She's got a college degree. She should be starting her career." And, "I could become a woman's national champion if I could go on Social Security and ski all the time." These hurt, but not enough to stop me or shame me.

I was lucky to be poor and ambitious, I guess. I supported myself with a meager $300-a-month Social Security disability income, which I supplemented with teaching skiing and whatever I could make writing. I had no disposable income: no money for lunches, sodas, gum, presents for friends, clothing, etc. But because I was brought up poor and lived on nothing as a child, where others might feel the sting of poverty, I felt the sting every morning of the cold air against my skin and reveled in my life here in the Colorado Rockies.

They were only five years, but the five most sacred in my life. Storyteller Clarissa Pinkola Estés says the soul can be scorched or bruised, but never broken, never destroyed as long as the person lives. However, the spirit is more vulnerable. It can be damaged and take quite a while to return to the body. Estés explains, "The spirit needs to be cajoled, propitiated..." In other words, it needs to be called back gently to the person's body to be trusted again.

Skiing did that for me. Five years earlier, my soul had been scorched by the brutal, ripping encounter with death. For a year, my soul shrank, then revived to deepen my character. But it took my spirit longer. It was on the mountain that my spirit rekindled. In 1977, several years after graduating college, I moved to Colorado. The first two years, I would wake every morning, and enter the Zen of Skiing. Whether it was a sunny, unseasonably warm December day, or a blizzard with bitter wind and cold — the thrill of ski on snow, speed under foot, graceful, gliding turns; or fast, hardly turning, headlong, barrel-for-the bottom runs — I could not stay home.

Once I was on the lift, instinct took over. No decisions. Which way to go once I got off the lift? I didn't think of it. I didn't know the mountain that well in those days, so each run was an adventure, a discovered treasure;

each day, different snow conditions; each day at different whims, I turned a different direction off the chair lift.

It wasn't just the physicality and freedom of skiing that fed my spirit. It was its social character. I found skiers a special breed. Perhaps the experience of having once been a beginner, a "fall-on-your-face, freeze-your-butt, I'm-never-coming-back, you-call-this-fun?" beginner, creates humility. Usually within a day, the person recovers and laughs and acknowledges that if others can do it, it can be done. Most skiers extend a hand to first-timers, and skiers know how to get over a bad day on the slopes with drink, song, and dance.

Calling out for a single in the chair lift line, I found skiing to be, ironically, a social-class equalizer. I found myself relating to doctors, lawyers, and CEOs as though we inhabited the same world. We shared at least one value: the love of the outdoors, playing in the snow. They spent a lot of money to ski. My license cost not an arm, but at least a leg as I skied under the blessing of Winter Park's free ticket for handicapped skiers who volunteered teaching. My income bracket was not a question to my chair lift compatriots, possibly just an assumption. For me the free ticket gave me not just a glimpse into a higher social class, but a chance to level the field. I was intelligent, literate and poor. I didn't feel the dissonance in these qualities on the slopes.

My Zen of Skiing lasted through at least two years of fun and freedom while I began my career as a journalist for the local paper. Then, in 1979, I reached a plateau of competence that left me hungry. In the late '70s, early '80s, the really good handicap skiers were self-taught. Not that talented, I turned in the direction of the best chance to improve: ski racing.

I might just as well use the Garden of Eden metaphor with ski racing as I have Zen with free skiing, because the rules, the exact times, the "never being good enough unless you win" aspects of ski racing introduced an element to my once holy, joyful, loving ski world: suffering.

Gone were the meandering mornings, whimsical trips off the chair lift to unknown adventures. Racing demanded hard work, listening to male authority figures (coaches), showing up on time, skiing to one specific run and turning in one specific direction through a series of predefined "gates."

Competition was my focus from 1979 until 1982 when I sustained a knee injury. After that event, I decided to quit the ski bum life and get my master's degree. But first I had to make some peace with ski racing. When Dick Rambler at the bank offered to sponsor me, I decided to race one more national championship. But this time I would do it differently. No pushing, just taking it easy, going with the flow: Zen and the Art of Ski Racing.

The 1983 National Handicap Ski Championships were held at Squaw Valley, California. In one week, thirteen feet of snow fell, covering window wells and doorways with quilts of soft crystals, the outlines of the whole resort molded softly with snow like a white fairy tale wonderland. It snowed every day we were there, all day. One night after having ventured over the pass to a party, we were stranded by an avalanche. We had to wait until it was cleared and then inch forward through a blizzard, guided only by the outlines of the guardrails over the pass to our side of the Sierras.

I took my time in the mornings: croissants and coffee and riding the chair lift to places unknown. I focused on listening to my body, quitting when I felt tired or stressed. The third day, when I ran into another three-track skier — crazy Wayne from Jackson Hole, who was not there as a spectator — I hooked onto him to see the mountain from the wild side. After exploring the front face, Wayne took me to another part of the hill which I hadn't been exposed to. As we descended the lift, with no warning, Wayne took off to the left in a hollering hoot while I looked on in disbelief. There were about 16 inches of new snow, the pitch was about 60 degrees, and Wayne was this streaking burst of snow — ski invisible, outriggers riding shotgun down the chute.

"That I cannot do," I said to myself with resolve, proud to know my limits. I looked around. There was no turning to the right, just a cliff and some deadly trees. I glided left along the rim of a bowl looking for a less intimidating slope. When I spied one, I thought, "I just have to maneuver that tricky spot, pass between those two trees, and I'll be able to merge with that mogul field." The moguls were steep and deep, but unlike Wayne's Way, bumps have a discernible bottom.

Drifting my ski into the fall line, I schussed between the two trees and reached the run. There I panicked. These were Volkswagen-size bumps. All I could think about was my knee, and my injury the previous year. In March of 1982, after intensive training and fatigue, stressed about competition, I had pushed myself beyond my limits just free skiing. I had shoved off a catwalk onto a mogul field and torn the ligaments in my knee. My only remaining knee. The type of snow I'd been caught by was referred to as "Sierra cement," a wetter snow than the Rocky Mountains' usual powder. Here I was again in the real thing.

My knee injury had happened two days before I was supposed to go to Switzerland for the 1992 World Championship Games; thus, I never got the chance to prove or measure myself against past performances, nor did I see the fruits of my season's training. This made a more profound impression than your average once-in-a-lifetime ski injury. Sitting on that mogul field, I was fearful of hurting myself again, yet I really believed I had a shot at winning the giant slalom at the nationals if I just relaxed.

To put things in perspective, I tried to imagine the worst thing that could happen. The worst was not re-injury but rehabilitation. I remembered the seven weeks in a wheelchair, with my only leg in a cast, imprisoned in my mountain mobile home, where the snow doesn't melt until April. My whole body groaned.

At first I chastised myself for not training with all the others on the hill the race was on, but Zen and the Art of Ski Racing wasn't about rigidity or rules or competition. That was a thing of my past. Zen was about following the flow.

Quieting my heart, leaning into the trough of the two-foot-high range of geodesic moguls, I judged the distance. How many consecutive turns would I have to crank until the run gave way to some knee-saving cruising?

"Go for it!" urged my wild side.

I balked. Was I turning into a scaredey cat? "But my knee. I'm afraid about my knee."

"Well then go halfway and stop, but don't psyche yourself out." Unfortunately fear overrode reason. I continued to sit there, and eventually I was paralyzed. I couldn't picture going down the hill on my rear; that would be too humiliating. Of course, if nobody saw it...

I looked uphill. At the top of the rim, from practically a cornice, three men inspected the run. One called down to me, "Are you all right?"

Good question, I thought. I yelled back. "I look down there," I paused, and pointing downhill, I said, "and all I see is danger."

His reply made my day. "Nothin' wrong with your eyes, Darlin'," and with that remark echoing in the air, he — and who I learned later were his two sons-in-law — twisted their way down the hill, huffing and puffing by the time they reached me.

I tried to not sound like Little Bo Peep. "I hurt my knee last season, and I think I'm psyched out."

"Follow us then." And he was off for this last gulley of bumps before the run-out. Practicing a technique my friend Fred called "linked recoveries," I followed their line and spent several more runs riding the lifts with them, learning about his two daughters and the present he gives them once a year: He takes their husbands on a ski trip. I love the people I meet skiing.

I didn't take the gold that year, but I was happy with my silvers. I lost the giant slalom to the Canadian Women's Nationals champion (I couldn't complain; I took a Canadian gold medal a previous year at their nationals), and I took second to Martha Hill in the slalom. Fingering the medals around my neck at the awards ceremony, I congratulated myself on a veritable "comeback" even if nobody else did. I'd put the Zen in ski racing.

More importantly, I'd gotten back to what skiing was all about: falling down and getting back up again, meeting fear and conquering it, discovering other people and God's good earth. Who could ask for a better five-year holiday?

1980, Geilo. Racing in Norway at the World Disabled Olympic Games.

2nd. Olympic Winter Games for Disabled

GEILO 1980 FEBRUARY 1st. — 7th.

2nd. OLYMPIC
WINTER GAMES
FOR DISABLED

GEILO

NORWAY
1980

Geilo ski area, where the 1980 Olympic Winter Games for Disabled were held.

Program for de
2. Olympiske Vinterleker
for Handicappede

KR. 10

GEILO 1.–7. FEBRUAR 1980

FOTO: JAN GREVE

2nd. OLYMPIC
WINTER GAMES
FOR DISABLED

NORWAY
1980

1980. A disabled competitor on the ice in Norway graces the cover of the brochure for the 1980 Olympic Winter Games for Disabled.

Geilo Remembered

(1989 Winter Park Manifest, revised 2002)

Ten years ago Winter Park was my hometown. It was a good town to be from if you were a handicap skier with the dream of becoming a competitive athlete. There was no organized team or coaches or even a competition center as we knew it, but Hal O'Leary had a handicap ski program, and the Rocky Mountain chapter of National Handicapped Sports skied here. (Among RMHSA were several of the Vietnam veterans who helped organize the Handicap National Championships.) If there was ever going to be a U.S. team, I figured it would start in Winter Park. I felt like a pioneer in three-track skiing when our first sanctioned team was born.

I am not a historian but a writer of autobiography; still, I knew of only two other international disabled winter sports events that preceded mine. One was a World Championship event at Grand Bornand, France; Debbie Phillips, a fearless three-track skier was one of the best in a contingent of New Englanders who took part, and one of the best in the world in 1978. Danny Pufpaff, my teammate and later coach, was also there along with a group of skiers from the Rocky Mountain group. The second event was the Olympics for Disabled in 1976 in Sweden that was attended by only one American, Bill Hovanik. Bill told me that when he went to the registration table in Salen, Sweden, he was asked what country he represented.

"United States," Bill replied.

143

"Are you the coach?"

Bill said yes, and when they asked him where his team was he told them, "I am the team."

After the first race the same man asked him how the United States had done. "The coach is very pissed at the team," was Bill's retort.

It wasn't until 1980 that the United States brought its first sanctioned group of athletes to the Olympic Games for the Disabled in Geilo, Norway. The Olympic National Committee for disabled skiing must have been made up of veterans of war; why else would they allow only amputees (once able bodied, while not those with diseases like cerebral palsy and polio) to race with outriggers? In 1980 we brought an exhibition team, including our best male and female three-track skiers: Debbie, who had a congenital defect, and David Jamison, post polio, as well as a four-tracker and a sit-skier.

That year, Winter Park was the U.S. disabled team's headquarters. The local newspaper, *The Winter Park Manifest*, featured stories on the local heroes. Deno Kutrumbos hosted a steak-dinner training table for the whole U.S. team at the Swiss House Tavern just before we left town.

I remember the endless backache and boredom of waiting at the Chicago and New York airports, and the struggles I had with my baggage in Norway when we arrived. It was hard enough being a gimp traveling abroad, but being a female expected to carry her weight equal to the men, I cursed my lack of Sherpa personnel and the lack of chivalry among some of my teammates. It's funny looking back and admitting the silly things I remember about being in the hotel in Oslo: the lack of familiar comfort foods, the distinctive ring of foreign telephones ("You chirped?" the first time I answered the phone), the phantom pain that never let up, the feeling I was competing to just keep up with the other gimps, and the asthma attack I suffered the first night, allergic to the down comforters and pillows.

A few days after we arrived, we were received by the King and Queen of Norway in a huge reception hall, and we stayed in Oslo for a week, alternately training in the surrounding ski towns and sightseeing in the city. I must confess I enjoyed the latter more than the former. I was awed by the gigantic museum where the Viking Ships were displayed, while I loved the Kon-Tiki exhibit and the history of these seafaring people.

I'll always cherish my memories of Norway, though some were tough to take at the time. At Norfiell, for instance, instead of a chair lift there was a poma lift, which is like a rope tow with a disk you put between your thighs. Pat Campanella, a Winter Park volunteer, just happened to be working in Norway that year. (When we first came to Norfiell, we saw a sign saying, "Colorado spoken here.") If it weren't for the coincidence that this Winter Park volunteer was the lift operator that day, I don't know what I would have done. Without a hip or pelvis on my left side, there was nothing to put the poma disk between — except the crook of my arm. I tried first to ride the lift to the top hanging on like that, and then I bailed when my arm muscles gave out. So I had no choice but to side-step up the rest of the way to reach the U.S. training gates. I was exhausted after the second run. Pat worked out the tricky maneuver of putting the poma "disk" between his legs. I would then jump in front of him — all this had to be done with perfect, quick timing — then lean against his legs all the way up the hill.

I quit training early that day out of sheer frustration. I felt at a bitter disadvantage to the AKs and BKs who could handle the lift and was angry this "accessibility" issue concerned no one but me. However, when I found the nearest bar, who should I find but two other Americans, Doug Kiel, our only arm and leg amputee, and Alan Hayes, a Vietnam vet and double AK amputee. I don't know if we were considered the Special Forces or not, but I didn't feel so alone after that.

When we finally said goodbye to the city of Oslo, we shared a train ride with several European teams, one of whom brought along an accordion player, and there was great cheer and musical accompaniment as we rode past the evergreen forests of Norway's countryside. When we got to Geilo, we were treated like celebrities. Our train was met by a parade of townspeople, including several huge trolls, the Norwegians' mythical "mascot." In our race packets we each received hand-drawn pictures from school children of each child's idea of an event at the Disabled Olympics.

We stayed at one of the classiest lodges I had ever seen, a rambling white mansion with a back door you could ski right up to, a garage out back where you could work on skis, a disco in the cellar, and a bar that was regularly attended by Americans and Japanese, who shared the same hotel. We were constantly greeted with "O-hio" or "Hi-hi!" or toasts of aquavitae. Huge smorgasbords were laid out for breakfast, lunch and dinner, and we were served sit-down style at lunchtime between morning and afternoon on the hill. The chicken cordon-bleu and huge slabs of cheeses, every type of fish known to water, and desserts that defied seconds, are but savory examples of the daily fare I remember as vividly as the Norwegian poma lift.

The Holmes lodge had been chosen for us earlier in the season by two Norwegians living in Colorado. Jerry Groswold, the president of Winter Park Resort Association, was the U.S. Disabled Ski Team's captain and Otto Tschudi, Winter Park's director of skiing, was a world-class pro ski racer who grew up skiing at his family's resort, Norfiel, Norway.

On the first day of "De 2.Olympiske Vinterlaker Handicapede," as the Norwegians called it, we took buses down to the massive arena where the festivities began. There was much pomp and circumstance and national pride as all the teams lined up with flags and were introduced and marched into the ceremony area. A special theme song had been written for the event. I recall that demonstrations of native dancing were performed after the awards, including square dancing in wheelchairs, but I don't recall that theme song. I do recall the town of Geilo.

Norway is very dark and cold in the winter. In Geilo the sidewalks were snow-packed, much more than Oslo. People rode wooden "sleds" — a chair seat with handles at the top, and two long steel runners on the legs. People rode with one foot on the runner, pushing off the snow with the other foot. Many sleds were trustingly left outside a shop with grocery bags tied to the handles and bundled-up kids on the seats. On the days when we didn't race, some athletes went to the outdoor rink to watch the curling and adaptive sports done on sleds. Others walked into town to the bakery and the gift stores. I bought pewter, carved wood, wool headbands and sweaters, and other finely crafted presents to bring back to my sponsors and the well-wishers from my Colorado hometown who pressed $50 bills into my hand before I left. I loved trading shopping tips with "The B Team," who were the wives of several of the male teammates.

Then there were the races. The race course for the giant slalom was much like a run at Winter Park. It was the weather that was unfamiliar. It was so cold our team photographer's camera froze up and we have no pictures of that first day. I think it was 26 below and humid. When we paired up on the chair lift, men from the Norwegian National Guard put army blankets over us. At the bottom of the course it was so cold we would watch for "eina minuten," — the word for "one minute" was announced in five languages — and then left the viewing area to warm up inside large green army tents with fires burning inside.

I had been the only American female three-tracker who didn't wipe out in the giant slalom, and the look on my teammates' faces when I made it past the slick turn and into the finish line induced a high I'll always remember. My run was good enough for eighth place. We had been somewhat humbled by the level of ski racers in Europe, especially the three-trackers. It was the beginning of the American resolve to get better training. I didn't know how to feel about my performance; however, the day was made a golden memory when, afterward, a Japanese man ran over to present me with a gift in a brown velvet pouch that said HJS. Inside was a beautiful silver pendant with a handicap skier etched on the front. After he saw my delight, he ran back to the Japanese team, and I wondered: Who could he be? And why me? I was told later he was Fukahara, the Japanese moviemaker who had filmed "The Man Who Skied Everest" and who remembered me from when he filmed the Japanese Handicap Ski Team's visit to Banff for the Canadian International Ski Games in 1976.

I remember the team meeting the morning after the giant slalom when our team gathered, obviously dejected. Team Captain Jerry Groswold, sensing the mood, remarked, "You are all winners." I could see the disdainful looks from the veterans, for whom the competition was a measure of the country for whom they had sacrificed so much. "No losers." I said. When he started to protest, I added, "Technically speaking." That got a few laughs. Every year since 1980 the United States has dominated the world competitions, including the Paralympics, which are now held the same year and same place as the Olympics for able-bodied athletes. The U.S. veterans made this possible.

Several days later, the slalom was an adventure with an entirely different tone. The course was very long, technical and somewhat flat. It was on a different part of the mountain, where you had to ski through ungroomed trails to get to the start. It was warm enough that day to watch the races from the bottom, so there was quite a crowd. The level of technical skill of the Austrian, German and Swiss racers was a revelation to many of the onlookers. The show put on by the athletes was awesome, not a popularized word then.

I was more nervous that day than I had been for the giant slalom, and the phantom pain level was jacked up to match my state of mind. Late for the bus, I cursed as I struggled on crutches to carry my outriggers until one of the arm amputees, Bill Dean, extended his kindness and carried them for me. He rode the chair with me, and as we skied to the start, I remember falling down every third turn and Bill, sticking by me, saying something like, "Remember: turn high, stay low, and stand up," as we approached the start. "Stand low, stay high and turn up?" I repeated silently, psyched out into a stupor.

I wasn't too happy with my time (eighth place), but I was proud to watch Diana Golden and Patty Werner come in at fifth and sixth places, beating a few of the amazing Austrian, Swiss and German women. Both Patty and Diana, ten years my juniors, went on to even greater glories, but 1980 was to be my last competition abroad. Though I coveted and trained for winning the downhill event in the next world championships, I was retired after a knee injury three days before our team left for Switzerland in 1982. Winter Park was a good town to recover in, since the Winter Park race team allowed me to watch the National Handicap competition in their training shack, up close and personal.

In February of 1990 athletes from all over the world were slated to leave their hometown hills to compete in Winter Park. When I first heard that Winter Park would host the first world class competition in North America, I was in grad school in Boston. A passion for my old home town burned in my heart. Leaving my advisor shaking his head, I arranged to do my graduate courses in absentia. Since I was also studying desktop publishing, I packed up my computer and returned to Winter Park for the 1989-90 ski season. I had no idea how I would make a living, but I needed to be among my kind and participate in whatever way I could. What a blast!

It's a long story, how I came to be a witness, a daily reporter, editor and publisher, at the first international games in the United States in 1990. With the help of a dozen French, German and English volunteers, I produced an eight-page newsletter with individual and national standings, and hard sports and human interest stories about the competition for the two weeks Winter Park hosted the games. I am so proud to have been trained as a racer and a journalist in the best hometown ski resort in the world.

The pendant given to me by Fukahara

1980 U.S. Disabled Ski Team posing at Winter Park before going to the Winter Olympic Games in Norway. Far Right: Team Captain Jerry Groswold.

1980. Very cold day for skiing in Winter Park. Photo by Bruce Benedict.

Real Gimps

(1985 *Caleidescope Mobility Magazine*)

We all joke around about the relative levels of disability. Above-the-knee amputees (AKs) will have a laugh about below-the-knee amputees: "BKs are almost human." But let's face it. Sometimes even a BK feels like a real gimp.

I once met a freestyle skier who had blown out her knee the previous season and was three-tracking during her convalescence. She liked it so much she started to call herself handicapped.

She beamed with pride when a pokey normie pointed her out wistfully to his partner. "Aren't those handicap skiers something?" She got free ski boots and cut the lift lines at Winter Park. She asked Hal O'Leary to sign her up for the Handicap Nationals. Hal told her she wasn't a gimp; she was a normie with an athletic injury, but somehow she found something so gratifying in being called handicapped she preferred this ignominious title rest of us earned by default.

When she told me one day that she could already feel the phantom pain starting, I knew her identity crisis was getting out of hand. I tried to explain that before you could be told that the pain you were feeling wasn't real — but phantom — you had to have lost a limb. But she didn't understand. So, here's to you, Kit. How do you know if you're a real gimp?

Real gimps can't run, can't do flutter kicks, don't stand on both legs in the shower and have at least one foot in the grave — and the other in a Dr. Scholl, or Birkenstock, or some other "good" shoe.

Real gimps can't stand stairs; they don't like high barstools where you can't bend your knee and rest your foot at the same time, and real gimps never turn down an offer to "take a load off?" "put your feet up?" or "give you a short lift to the gas station with that can, buddy?"

Real gimps get nervous around ladders and wooden-planked piers. Real gimps walk real carefully over slippery tile.

Gaining a few pounds is no small problem to a real gimp.

A real gimp has an aversion to the expression "pre-existing condition" on the lips of insurance men.

Fiberglass and hairdryers are not an unlikely combination to a real gimp — who often has had to repair an artificial limb in an emergency.

Real gimps always have more luggage to carry at the airport than their able-bodied companions. And they actually carry less of it. No one can resist offering a hand to someone without a leg.

Real gimps know what it means to get hurt and not merely get better, but to get hurt and live.

A gimp's greatest privilege is a driver's license and a handicapped plate.

Real gimps hate x-rays, scalpels, needles and doctors who say, "I've never worked on anybody like you before." But real gimps love nurses; they're the ones who really care.

The phrase, "Better living through chemistry," may have been coined by Dupont, but it lives on the lips of the real gimp.

A real gimp will never turn down a massage. Real gimps spend more money on medical and prosthetic expenses than businessmen on lunches and recreation.

Real gimps have been known to become prosthetists just to reverse the financial odds.

Real gimps always carry a spare ace bandage or a spare pair of crutches in the car.

In response to the question "What happened to you?" real gimps have at least one truthful answer, one technical explanation, and one creative lie. Possible consecutive answers might be in order of question: "Motorcycle accident." "Pseudomonas gangrene infection and subsequent amputation of left limb." And "A shark bit me."

Taking off a leg in company is almost as natural for a real gimp as taking off a tie or belt.

If you've gotten real great at one sport simply because you can't do any others gracefully, you're a real gimp

Now there may be many of you out there reading this who thought you were real gimps simply because you could show somebody like Kit that you were different. You take off your artificial leg and show her the difference between an athletic injury and a stump. But if you can say none of the above, you are not a real gimp.

You are what we real gimps call a "supergimp."

Irene Dogmatic's version of me being sent to the bottom of the river.

The S.S. Ego

(1980 *Caleidescope, Winter Park Manifest*)

The Sunday of Memorial Day weekend was sunny but cool and windy, the whitecapped Colorado River running fast and high. Seven of us Fraser Valley-ites were out for an impromptu expedition on the river.

I'm not saying it was a slipshod operation, but right from the start at the pump house loading spot, our crew was a little different. While several groups of rafters wearing yellow raingear and wetsuits loaded up their eight-oar rigged 12-man silver blimp rafts, we seven stood around a gray, 25-year-old, four-man Navy Surplus raft named the S.S. *Ego*.

Our skipper, Andy Miller, leaned over the S.S. *Ego* with a can of adhesive tape patching the vessel's two known holes. He was mentioning how glad he was we had got the pump fixed. Not that he minded blowing up the raft on his own steam, he said, it was just less embarrassing this way.

The S.S. *Ego*, we learned, was named for its propensity to deflate.

When the Ego was puffed up properly, our two-man, two-woman crew jumped in and headed off. Two of the guys remaining, who were promised rides after the girls' turn, drove the dry clothes, tuna fish and the truck down to Radium to rendezvous.

Our Seventh Son, James Miller the Kayaker, looking like just another insect on the river, had already tipped his pointy yellow nose off the bank and was maneuvering around Nelson Eddies and slithering into the marsh-like hinterlands with that great ease of movement kayakers command. Like a horseman and his mount, a kayaker and his vessel are truly one.

We dubbed James our token kayaker. Sleek and graceful, he glided all over the watery terrain, while we bulbous, balloon-sided rafters bobbed along the current, rather undirected in the gentle flow of this meandering stretch of water before the first set of rapids.

"Jane, if we should dump," Andy addressed the other female party on the raft, Jane Hansberry, with whom I've shared many excursions: "Keep your feet, er...foot, downstream and push off the rocks." Jane looked at me with distress.

"Don't worry, Jane. It won't tip," I reassured her. Jane, like myself, is an amputee, but she is always up for a challenge. I had been given the same warning the one other time I went rafting and felt the same terrible inadequacy of being a one-legged person in a two-legged river world. I still can't picture myself, with my vulnerable amputation, pushing off rocks with one foot. But I knew for a fact that when friends take a handicap friend rafting they are extra careful not to tip. They even secure your crutches to the boat, just in case, so you will know they have your every concern in mind.

I looked at my handmade, wooden, dear-to-my-heart crutches, laying loose in the boat, and asked Andy if maybe we should tie them down.

"Nah," Keith, our fourth mate, said. "I've got my knee on them, they're okay." Jane's wooden peg leg, which unscrews from a socket she wears, was also loose. Still, I knew we wouldn't tip because, basically, this stretch of the river from the pump house to Radium was easy.

We chit-chatted with our token kayaker in between his fickle affairs with eddies and then pulled over to a grassy bank to refuel; that is, we all got out of the raft and pumped more air in it. When we got back in and were pulled down to the nearest rapids, we felt buoyant with the extra pressure.

All of a sudden we are moving faster and faster and yoweee, whee! up and down, and thank God this only lasts for a short while! The raft undulated from tip to tail. Sitting in the back of the boat, I can see my friends in front up in the air, and then I'm up there looking down on them heading into a huge green wave. The first rapids were like a roller coaster on water.

"There's a sleeper up there on the right, Andy," Keith motioned, "and a big rock there we've got to watch out for." We made it by that one, and then, after a few more commands, it wasn't obvious to any of us, except maybe that smirking, practical joker of a river, that one of these guys' strokes was a little stronger and longer than the other's. So that's how I think we hit "The Hole." We banged it around in couplings of conversational theory for hours later, but everyone had his own version of why we hit The Hole and lost our crew.

Except for me, of course. Though no longer in the boat, I was never separated from it. Because no matter how many times I got dragged under and how many mouthfuls I swallowed, no matter how many waves whipped the boat in another direction, sometimes landing it on top of me, I had a mission and hung on. I had hold of a piece of rope on that raft, and I was convinced if I let go, I'd either get eaten up by another treacherous hole, or I would get dragged by a furious whip water wall all along a jagged, rock-bottomed river with not even a plastic sandal left on my one-and-only foot to protect me from the rushing destiny of bodily destruction.

Water swirled all around me, pulling me down and throwing me up, until I thought, "Please God, if I'm gonna have to go down the drain, why not in warm bath water?"

Lifetimes later, Andy, the air pump clutched to his chest like a heroic retriever, was alongside me, trying to get over the whale of sidewall into the raft. "Where the *@%+* is Jane?" he was yelling at me.

Behind us bobbed a brown head still wearing its Vuarnets, mouth opening and closing, but no sounds discernible from our 50-foot or so distance. She was irretrievable. Jeeze, I thought, her first time rafting.

Like a policeman when you need him, Keith appeared inside the raft, paddling furiously, apparently so stunned that he didn't see Andy and me, the two frozen, drowned rats hanging on to the side and each other as the S.S. *Ego* continued its rushing roller-coaster course through the canyon.

"Pull Cale in, Keith," Andy shouted, and, gasping for air like a hooked grouper, I landed with no finesse in the bottom of the boat.

Still stunned, I attempted with numbed body and soul to pull my comrade in with me. The three of us maneuvered over into the reeds at the side of the retreating rapids.

I have a real bad problem, which can be both antisocial and rude. Sometimes, in times of great sobriety, import or danger, I do not react appropriately. I looked up the river to where Jane was stranded. She was being directed by our omnipresent kayaking compatriot, James, to lay her body over the tail of the kayak, lean downstream, and he would tow her down to the raft. She tried leaning and slipped off and, just in time, she caught the loop at the tail end of the kayak and held on while James paddled precariously down to us.

I began to laugh hysterically. I did this once in Denver on Colorado Boulevard in rush-hour traffic when my car stalled in the passing lane, and a van pulled up behind me to help. Despite his warning flashes, four cars piled up behind him, banging bumpers and folding fenders, as the rear window of a Pinto catapulted from its mounting and smashed against the pavement.

God help me, I thought. Jane is still in that freezing cold river and I'm ready to split a seam. Trying to stifle the hysteria, I took deep breaths and began to shiver. Andy joined me, saying, "She's okay...banged up in the knee, but she's okay. Jeeze, Cale. Can you believe I held on to that pump? 'I've got to get the pump,' I was saying to myself, and all of a sudden I thought, 'What am I worrying about a goddamn pump for? I could die in this stuff!'"

It was no use. A giggle escaped first, then a chortle, and the next thing I remember is that as Keith and James carried Jane over to the raft, Andy and I were prostrate in the raft laughing so hee-hee-hee-hard we were crying.

"Can we help you?" Another raftsman yelled to us.

"Yeah," Keith responded. "Look for a crutch and a peg leg." Now we were all in hysterics.

"Hand me that paddle Keith, and I'll use it for a crutch," I said.

"Which one?" he asked.

"Oh, either oar," I said.

We lay frozen and shivering near the point of hyperventilation when the sun's warm rays began to be absorbed by the black rubber raft, calming us down to recollection of certain thrilling moments in the near drowning. We were all thankful for our life jackets, no matter how bulky and ridiculous they had seemed at the beginning of the trip. Jane had been in the water for more than five minutes, and was n-n-n-numb. We found her peg, sucked in by an air space on the bottom of the boat, when we tipped it over to empty out the water. My crutch was doubling as driftwood somewhere on the Colorado.

There was a drowning the next day on the same river over near Eagle. The man was not wearing a life jacket. But that's another story. There are a million stories in this naked river. This has been one of them.

1982, Arches National Park, Utah. The photographer Joanne Yankovich and I.

1998, "Here to Eternity Beach," Oahu, Hawaii. I hiked down steep lava rock stones to the bottom of a crater where a beautiful beach awaited those who made the effort.

Mermaid Adventure

(1997 *Howlings*)

On Martha's Vineyard in summer, sun worshippers crowd the long strips of ocean front, not many of whom venture far into the water on the open ocean side of the island; the surf is rough, and the waves crash to the shore creating a powerful undertow. Onshore, crutches holding down the edges of my blanket, I surveyed the scene.

The beach was confetti colorful, with radio-blasting blankets, multi-colored umbrellas, windsurfers, people running kites, seagulls flying overhead, and thickets smattered with roses behind the dunes. I was transfixed by the sea — the sparkle of water teased by wind, and always the mesmerizing motion of the heaving, breathing ocean.

I watched it rush to shore in transparent waves, the water gathering upon itself until a wall of wave formed, and then, seeming to hesitate for a second, one minuscule white drop tipped over the top, and the entire water wall from top to bottom curled over and rushed after it, skidding in every direction as foam covered the shore.

That was where the action was. I wanted to be there. Watching from my blanket, resting on my elbows, I began to feel more like a mermaid than a primate.

Since I have only one leg, the only way to get out there was to crutch, planting one at a time until I was past the breaker waves. Once in the sea beyond the crashing surf, I moved around freely, water balancing me as air never could. I could almost give up my crutches were it not for my return to land. But, because I had to hang onto them, I envisioned my crutches as a portable wooden raft. Lying down, bobbing in the deep water, I held them across my chest lengthwise and was carried forward by the surge of swells. It was like being rocked by your mother at birth: So gentle. And peaceful. And rhythmic. And dependable.

Unless your mother dropped you.

Which is what happened when one wave bore me so far inland I ended up reeling in the roiling surf, wave-thrashed and bashed, slapped around and agitated, water amok, undertow sucking me into the next crest. I had a firm grip on my crutches. I knew the consequences of losing one, having already donated a beautiful hand-carved crutch to the Colorado River during my rafting adventure.

Though only thigh-deep in water, I nearly drowned. Spitting out salt water, I couldn't get my leg under my body at the same time as I got my head over the water; then, as I finally got some footing, I struggled to get the crutches in position at my side. I planted a few steps out of the buffeting surf, and as I did so, I looked down and realized the top of my two-piece bathing suit was around my waist.

Oh, no! I quickly ducked under the water in a crouch and backed into the surf past the breaking waves again. I thought for a split second: I hate to let go of my crutch, but I will not walk bare-breasted out of the surf for everyone to see, no matter how gorgeous my breasts might be. I pulled up the suit, and the next second reached back down for the crutch, and in that infinitesimal passage of time, the Atlantic Ocean appropriated my most necessary prop in life.

Oh, no! I tried walking back to shore with one crutch, but the waves were too strong. I retreated to the deep waves and contemplated.

What to do? My last resort in any crisis is to ask someone to help me, and I soon determined that this was my only option. I spied a man onshore gazing my way, and I waved out to him with my now-free other arm, singing out, "Oh, excuse me, sir, do you think you could give me a hand?" Actually, what I needed was another leg...

He came out as though he knew what was going to happen next. He must have been watching me for a while. "Sure," he said. "How do you want to do this?"

We tried my walking with one crutch at my side and him bracing me on the other, but the surging water was too strong for both of us. I could have suggested he carry me out like a real mermaid, but I was feeling a curious desire to be amphibian just then, able to negotiate both land and sea. Because I didn't want to be carried out in his arms like a baby or a bride, I opted for another arrangement. "Maybe you could give me a piggyback," I suggested.

He bent down, and I climbed on, my arms around his neck, and in the next five minutes we enacted a hysterical scene, as I slipped and slid off his well-oiled, suntanned back. Unable to straddle him, at first I'd slip to the right. Then, unable to get a grip around his waist, my weight would shift and I'd slip to the left, and I wondered, how do mermaids do it, anyway? Finally I just dangled, and he high-stepped through the surf. We both laughed while he bore me ashore, the smiles on our faces easing my embarrassment. He acted as if this act of heroism was an everyday occurrence and set me down lightly on my blanket.

The crutch: Where could it have gone? He went back to look, but I knew it would probably be deadwood by the time it washed ashore on the New Jersey coast. He helped me by finding a piece of driftwood as long as a cane, and I thanked him, having no idea at the time how I was going to get to my car with this stick.

I got a great tan that day, because to save face, I waited until most people left the beach around 3 p.m. It wasn't a pretty sight, but I made it to the car with the gnarled stick in my hand and the remaining crutch under my arm. Once in my car I felt nearly human after this flirtation with the sea. I never felt so grounded as on this ride to town to find new crutches. Ten dollars short, I might have had to hit every yard sale in town if the drug store I'd hopped into hadn't had a second-hand pair they sold me for $16. Lucky.

I still have my mermaid moments, and I still venture into the rough sea. However, I now keep a spare pair of crutches in my car.

And I always wear a one-piece suit in the surf.

1998, "Here to Eternity Beach," Oahu, Hawaii.

Top: "I'd rather be soaring!" Posing at the Waitsfield, Vermont, airport. Bottom: 1982, Mike Murphy and I prepare for takeoff in his glider plane at Waitsfield Airport, same day.

Airports: Bags and Bones
(1995)

Traveling with a disability is a tricky business, each disability presenting its own unique set of problems. My problem traveling in general is that sitting exacerbates a chronic pain condition; a long flight with my artificial leg on is impossible. Instead of wearing my prosthesis, I carry it in a large wardrobe bag and wear a little "bucket" prosthesis I call a "butt." Once I'm on the airplane I try to scout out an empty seat and convince my seatmate that he or she would really be helping me if they would move to that unoccupied seat. That way I can get horizontal.

I don't always get lucky, though. When I travel with a friend, it's a little easier, depending on the friend. These days I buy two seats and put my leg across my friend's lap. I remember the first time I flew with my one-time boyfriend Paul. I told him in advance, "Traveling with me is a trip in itself." Paul didn't tell me about his fear of flying.

A plane is the only place I go where I can't keep my crutches stored at my side. The flight attendant will notify me that in case of possible airline disaster, or even mere turbulence, they have to be stored with the carry-on luggage in overhead compartments. I don't like it much, especially if I want to leave quickly for the lavatory, but it's part of the trade-off for traveling with a disability.

Paul, always protective of my freedom and mobility, was not as forgiving as I. A little black cloud formed above his head when the flight attendant asked for my crutches so she could lock them above.

"All seat belts fastened. Prepare for takeoff," I heard the pilot announce while I stretched my back slowly and deeply, inching my arms and then my head forward to the floor. I needed a good stretch before the flight took its toll on my back. My head was completely to the floor, which must have looked rather odd.

When the attendant came by, checking seat belts row to row, she stopped and said to Paul, "What's that?" She pointed to my back.

"What do you mean?" I could hear him say testily. He was still teed off about the crutches.

"Who does that belong to?" her finger wagged.

"It's my girlfriend," he said.

"It's your girlfriend's?" she asked.

"No. It *is* my girlfriend," he said between clenched teeth.

"Oh!" I heard her say with fright. "Is she all right?"

"No, she's in pain," he said crabbily, obviously irritated that we were the subject of her attention again. I heard their exchange while I was stretching, and I thought, "Now, why did he have to say that?" The fact I have chronic back and phantom limb pain is a hidden handicap I'd rather keep concealed; it can create a crisis out of a normal, everyday situation.

I heard her say then, in a high, nasal tone, "I'm sorry. I thought she was a duffel bag!"

I have encountered many "attitudinal barriers" as a person with a disability, but I'd never before been mistaken for a duffel bag. I was smiling as I sat up to catch her eyes and say "I'm okay," and also to help her laugh a little at herself, since everyone around us had heard her. I smiled broadly while I met her eyes.

"I'm sorry," she said, batting her eyelashes, and then repeated herself, this time stretching her voice further when she saw my face, "I thought you were a duffel bag!" A few people around us snickered, and she was still serious enough to make me squirm. Paul was finally chuckling. He wouldn't be for long.

After the flight comes the baggage struggle. Because I have a high amputation that requires plastic, corset-like attachments around my torso to hold the leg on, I have a really strange-looking wardrobe bag.

At the Denver airport, rather than a wheelchair waiting for me, the airlines provided a utility cart to take arrivals to the baggage area. However, once I was seated in the cart, the porter informed us that this service was just for the handicapped; Paul would not be allowed to go with me. So much for mainstreaming the handicapped, I thought. Paul stood up slowly. He was already loaded down with our take-on luggage and his guitar and my garment bag, so I suggested we let all our "stuff" ride with me. Keeping his guitar, he loaded the other bags and began walking to the baggage claim, the little black cloud reappearing.

When the porter loaded the garment bag onto the back, he said to me, "What's this? This your bone?" He had a Jamaican accent.

"I'm sorry," I said, "What did you say?"

"Is this your 'bone'?" he repeated.

People have called my prosthesis many things, but this was the most ridiculous. Perhaps because he wasn't a native speaker, the closest he could get to orthopedic appliance was "bone"? I mused. This was right up there with the time a police officer, noticing my artificial leg, addressed me as "Peg."

I laughed inwardly while we rode to baggage, looking forward to telling Paul, who was by now far behind. When we got to the elevators, the man expected Paul to be behind us in order to take me the rest of the way, but Paul had taken the escalators to the baggage area. The porter then got in the elevator and left me upstairs. I was speechless. What am I, a piece of luggage?

When Paul spotted the man at the baggage area without me, he asked where I was.

"She can't come down," the man said with concern, Paul later told me.

"She can come down," Paul informed him, as though the man thought I was an invalid.

"She couldn't leave her "bone," the man said.

"What!" Paul said with exasperation.

With a musician's reverence, the man exclaimed, "She couldn't leave her trombone alone up there."

1977, Boston. Yoga posing for photographer Phil Miller.

Top: My father took out his teeth and wore a beret to look fabulously French-artist-like after being egged on to pose with the Revere Beach picture he painted for me from a 1940's postcard. Bottom: 1982, posing with Dad.

Daddy

(1997 *Howlings,* revised 2002)

My Dad was a child. Of the universe, of God, of my mother's, of his mother's, of mine. He was my dad, but he was like a child.

My Dad wasn't a sporty man. He wore suit coats and ties in public places. He was tall and lanky and danced like a sailor with his sea legs balancing below him.

When we were little he called us "mein kinder" and playfully tossed us in the air like circus tumblers. He taught us Pig Latin, and said prayers with us in real Latin. "Pater Noster," he recited on bended knees, hands clasped over the bed, his dark, wavy hair stealing in front of his eyes, he winked as he peeked over his folded hands to see us giggling. While he recited the Lord's Prayer in the vulgate, we four little tow-heads, Billy, Chrissie, Kathleen and I, had joined in with delicious, silly gibberish. This blasphemy maddened my mother, but we loved our father's clowning and his special talents. He was an artist, a joker, a linguist.

My dad, I learned growing up, was not a proper adult, though. He didn't behave as adults do. There was something wrong with my daddy. Grandpa said he was a loser. Not my dad, I thought. My mother explained Dad was sick. I learned later Dad had a mental illness, schizophrenia.

Daddy painted pictures in oil, a huge canvas of me when I was three. The photographer posed me on a stool in the studio, but in the picture Daddy painted I was sitting on a mushroom in a garden. The painting was huge, 6' x 4', and he had painted many smaller canvases of each of us children and our cousins.

Dad was naturally musical, and each instrument we learned as children (Chris, piano; me, accordion; and Billy, trumpet) he borrowed outside our practice time teaching himself to play. He mastered accordion and trumpet, inspiring us with his enthusiasm.

Daddy knew the punch lines to all the jokes on television, and he asked us funny riddles like: what's black and white and red all over? A newspaper! He could speak German and French. He was also a ham radio operator, and when voices came in from Russia, Germany, and France, he could translate the gist for us.

Navy men, he and his younger brother, Uncle Bob, spoke the Morse code to each other when they didn't want us to know their business.

"Dit-diddle-da-da. Dit-dit-dit," Daddy said, leaning forward in his armchair. Uncle Bob, fired back with his dit-diddle-da-das as he reclined on the couch, his legs crossed in the air and one toe pointing to the ceiling, his hand resting on one knee with his cigarette held up. We in turn tried to jumble their messages by yelling our own versions: "Dit-dit-dit-da-da-da!," I jumped in after Daddy finished his piece, before Uncle Bob could respond. Looking back, they may never have been coding a single English word, but I felt like we were on the submarines with them, spies decoding enemy information.

I remembered Daddy dancing me on his feet, our hands interlocked; I remember him giving me piggybacks to bed. I remember the thrill of receiving and opening one of his letters when I was away with Nana over the summer. "Mein Kinder," it began, and he drew pictures of bunny rabbits, kangaroos, and a picture of me sitting on a lily pad. I was proud of my daddy and I felt loved.

But he changed when I was ten and our sister Kathleen died. While dad was out of work and babysitting us, Ma worked double shift through the night, and apparently her absense from home ended their intimacy. Or at least that's one excuse for why, a few years later, my father turned his attentions toward me. When my mother said I couldn't wear nylon stockings like all the other girls in seventh grade, I moaned about it to Dad, who said sit on his lap, so I did, and for some strange reason he then gave me money to buy a pair of stockings.

As a young adult, I learned the dark side about my dad's disease, and much of his behavior had to be kept a family secret, even after he was sent to a home for mentally ill and alcoholic men. But you could still tell he was not quite right. He once told a boyfriend of mine, "She was such a sexy baby."

One day I was driving him from the hospital home to visit us, he was apparently hallucinating voices. "Who are these artists who are doing these things to you?" he asked.

"I didn't say a thing, Dad," I said, instantly on alert.

"You must have been thinking it, then," he said to my alarm. "Your mother used to always do that to me."

I thought a while and said patiently, "No. I was looking at that yield sign and thinking I better slow down." That was the moment I realized why my mother was such a wreck during my whole childhood.

After I lost my leg, one of the first things he said when he came to see me was: "Didn't I tell you to stay away from those motorcycles?" and a few years later Dad asked me if I had any dates. "Do they go much for handicappers these days?" he said, sensitive as ever. "They didn't in my time."

Once he could get on his own, living with Uncle Bob, Dad was allowed to visit us whenever he wanted. He and Uncle Bob were even expected for the holidays. He had many opportunities, but my father took no responsibility for the lifetime of trouble and hurt a father does to a girl child when he sexualizes her, whether he actually touches her or not, whether he did it with full consciousness or in a psychotic state. (What he did to the boys is another matter.) When I walked by him in my own living room, I was forced to deny my body, cave my chest in, and crawl out of my skin while my mind huddled in a corner of the ceiling. I remember the strange feeling of betrayal I felt when I saw him with my two sisters, one under each arm, who didn't remember anything about the awful years. He used to tell me I was his favorite; he now told each of them individually they were his favorite. So I was also jealous. I was thinking, he's better now. Instead of being concerned for them, I felt cheated.

Our family perpetrated a gag-order of denial over those years in order to keep Dad in the family. By the little kids' teens, Ma had a good job, and Dad was even invited on an outing. We would all take a ferry boat with her, Uncle Bob, and Dad from Rowe's Wharf in Boston to Nantasket Beach on the south shore, like we used to do before Kathleen got sick. It became a yearly tradition, even after Ma died. One thing our mother wanted more than anything was for us to be a family who stays together and helps each other.

I think it was to honor her that every year, two decades later, we adult brothers and sisters still went with Dad at least once during the summer to Nantasket. We went on a Sunday when the Big Band music was played under the pavilion. All the old-timers gathered there to dance from 1 to 3. This was Dad's favorite part. Earlier while we built castles with the grand kids or waded in the ocean, he took his strolls on the boulevard, buying himself a coffee, having a few cigarettes, thinking about... math problems probably, or some other dilemma from the abstract universe he lived in. He generally stayed to himself, but when the band struck up, his toes would get tapping, he would get Ma out there to dance, or he'd call Suzy or Joanne or Chris or me to waltz or polka or swing dance until he wore out. Wheezing, coughing, and laughing.

He was in his glory, surrounded by his four daughters, a bevy of blonde beauties; we were vestiges of his World War II pin-up girl fantasies of what waited at home after the military action. He was never able to relate to his two male children, but he got along quite well with their wives.

He was out of breath a lot. He smoked. Do you know he quit smoking for seven days?! Joanne talked him into it. My Dad quit smoking for seven whole days. You have to have known my Dad, his life long addiction to coffee, cigarettes and cholesterol to appreciate this sign of spiritual progress.

He had terrible headaches. It wasn't like he cried "Wolf" so many times that when the wolf finally came we didn't believe him. But the last few weeks of his life, when he was so sick that he had Uncle Bob make the calls for him (Uncle Bob would say in his raspy voice and Boston accent, "Cah-rolyn, your fah-thah wants to talk to ya."), it wasn't like we didn't think he was really sick. It was more like he was always sick-with diverticulitis, emphysema, terrible sinus headaches-with his mental illness-and so when he had the flu and his back hurt, and his legs were numb, we just didn't think it was going to kill him. So no one rushed to his aid.

While a few of my siblings may comfort themselves with the fatalistic aphorism, "The Lord giveth and the Lord taketh away," I take refuge in statistics: He was just one individual of the 12 percent of the population that died the winter of 1988 from complications due to the flu. How could I have known? What could I have done?

It wasn't the funeral, but the half-eaten chocolate birthday cake that said "Feb 8" on it they found March 4th in his fridge that got to me. I didn't invite my Dad to my birthday party because it wasn't a family occasion. But I knew it would hurt him to not be included. But, he did invite me over to his house after my birthday, said he had something for me. How could I have known?

Walking through the dark, rusted iron door past cinder-blocked walls and stone steps that led to his apartment door, I dreaded seeing what the joint looked like now.

These housing project apartment buildings could fool you. From the outside, they promised cockroaches, stained walls and accumulated dirt of years of housekeeping neglect, but in the apartment across from Dad's, a lady named Evelyn, a drunkard, lived in shabby opulence. Her inner spare room was sepia-toned like an old photo or an opium den. Oriental rugs covered the cracked linoleum floor, and so many wood-framed photographs hung from the walls, you would never meet an open space long enough to be offended by it. She had big overstuffed chairs and small wooden cups resting on coffee tables at every elbow turn, and differently patterned draperies hung over windows and walls and in the doorways leading to other rooms. These other rooms we never saw. We only ever went to Evelyn's if, and when, our knock on Dad's door was unanswered and we thought my father might have gone over there to visit.

To say she was a friend of my dad's would be a misrepresentation. Dad was "familiar" with his acquaintances in a way that's hard to describe. Joanne's boyfriend Jack once characterized him as a perpetual teenager; fag hanging out the corner of his mouth in continual bravado, he spoke to perfect strangers in a conspiratorial tone: "How'ya doin' today, Jack?"-He called everybody Jack. "Gotta spare cigarette, Jack?"

"The old hag's half in the bag," he tells us in an aside. To Evelyn he says, "The kid's come around, I gotta go. Thanks for the phone." He puts his cigarette butts out in her cups and otherwise fouls her air as though it were his own.

Now, Dad's place, that was a dive. Straight to the bottom of the economic ladder-only one rung above homelessness. He lived with his brother Bob, a war vet with a mental disability checked by heavy doses of the drug Prolyxin. A few years before he died, Chris and I helped get Dad on Social Security when he could no longer keep up with his dishwashing job, the end of a career in electronics lost tragically to an illness he would not get treatment for. Just a few years ago, Joanne gave him a phone for Christmas, and she had been paying the bill ever since.

Even on the phone, he was overly familiar. "Please leave your message after the tone," my answering machine politely concluded, and then I'd hear that unmistakable swaggering growl: "Yahr-ritch-yah-fah-thah. Gimme a call sometime," was the mumbled message. Other times he didn't say who it was that called. "Call your father," the machine said.

Just before he died, he called me and said he was working on a picture of my mother; did I want it. "It doesn't look like her," I said of the half-finished canvas. He'd responded impatiently, "It looks enough like her." I'd seen it on his easel one of the last times I'd visited.

Today I look up close, and I want to cry. I didn't know my father had begun to wear glasses to see nearsighted. Next to a pair of glasses, one lens cracked, and his paints, is the framed picture he was using to paint my mother. He was painting her from a photo under glass so sticky with dust and grease that you could barely recognize her image beneath. I took the picture out, and sat down.

My mother's face smiles up at me in all her radiance. Now this looks like her.

I sit holding the picture, staring at the canvas. So my dad was losing his eyesight. How could I have known? He never said a word, and I never saw the glasses. Uncle Bob offers me some coffee. I ask, "Do you have anything cold?" There's beer, but he doesn't offer. He must be rationing his silver bullet cans. I take a drink of water from him and later ask for a swig of beer, which he gives me in a half-full, delicate china cup.

Finally I ask him. "Has anybody said anything about wanting that picture of Ma?" He grunts. Shuffles his feet.

"Nah, take it, Carolyn. It's yours. He woulda' wanted you to have it."

There on the easel is the picture of Ma, looking not yet like her, but a presence in any event because it was the last thing Dad was working on.

Driving home across the Charles River with the painting on the passenger seat, I weep a few tears of regret and guilt and sadness for the tragedy of my Dad's life. Oh, Daddy. You couldn't support your family. I understand why we were poor. But not why you let your wife work double time, and you abused your children, physically and sexually, rather than take a course of medications. I understand that these medications left your brother Bob a mess of embarrassing ticks and side effects that masked the man.

Oh, Dad. Thanks for the impressionist painting. I'm sorry I didn't come for the cake. I know it meant so much to you to have me kiss you hello, only toward the end I did not want to do that; it gave me the creeps. I know I had forgiven you for almost everything already. It's just that I am stuck between conflicting images. I can't seem to lay down my feelings of betrayal against the memory of my childhood's "Daddy."

Now I see that this is his legacy. I will always need to see the world from a different angle. I will always embrace the homeless man, always kiss the ugly frog. My vision needs to be not only a little out of focus, but also allow for a layer of grime in order to graciously receive the fruits of my father's talent, humor, and intelligence, which he passed on to his children, these god-given gifts of a parent with a mental illness, who could never grow up.

Peppi was the first dog I ever owned. He paved the way for Comet, who became my companion for life.

Peppi, the Cowboy Poodle

(1993 *Contest, Honorable Mention*)

They say that a dog is a man's best friend. You don't hear much conventional wisdom about women and their dogs. So I'm here to tell you: A girl's first dog is like her first boyfriend — unforgettable.

First, we fell in love. Peppi and I met at the Dumb Friends League. He was a five-year-old miniature black poodle whose back legs bowed like a cowboy's, and his grooming cut made him look like he was wearing a pair of chaps. Irresistible. I noticed he had a little smile, and then he peed in the corner of the visitor's room.

"He's marking his territory. Don't worry," the DFL worker reassured me. "They mostly do it outside." His territory: That must mean he likes me.

Then came the honeymoon. Peppi had just been neutered, but the hormones were still raging. So my first day with my new canine was much like hanging out with a 14-year-old boy at the onset of puberty. Peppi sniffed, licked, and humped everything in his new world, including me. Now, I'm not saying that my first boyfriend was like a dog, but there were some similarities in their hormonal orientation to their environments. In two days, however, the testosterone waned.

I loved to watch him move. With a spring in his step, he was always one romp or prance away from jumping into the air with happiness. After he pooped, he would stamp his

189

back feet like a bull and then jump into the air — even when he was on a leash that would yank him down rudely. He was one free-spirited guy.

It didn't take long for the honeymoon to wane. At some point when sharing the same space with a boyfriend, a girl can feel invaded. Peppi, who had been an outdoor dog for five years, was underfoot in my home from the first day. At all hours he followed me around the house. From the desk where he lay at my feet, he would uncurl from his comfortable dog-skin-rug position and follow me three feet away to the printer, watching every move I made. When I dropped a pencil or piece of paper, he interpreted this as my invitation to play and would rustle up the newly copied story or fetch the pen and chew on it until I would scold him, speaking in my incomprehensible tongue: "No. There's a difference between living in a yard and living in a home where you can listen to Van Morrison in a comfortable climate." He'd give me that stare I translated as, "Read my mind."

Women complain about housebreaking boyfriends, but with a dog, it's literal. The first night at 4 a.m., I was awakened by clinking dog tags. Thinking he must have to go potty, I began to put on my sock and boot — only to have him pull at both gleefully, as though we were really up for tug-of-war games. As soon as I pulled him off me and got to the room where I kept his leash...surprise! I found his droppings. The next day at 9 a.m. I discovered where he'd peed. My ex-backyard dog had never had to tell anyone when he had to go, so he just went about his own business, whenever, wherever. I bought a book about modifying animal behavior, and training began. Soon I would learn more fascinating details about his personal habits. I don't know which was more charming: checking for ear mites or checking stools for worms.

Living with someone can really kill the romance. With Peppi, the immediate intimacy of grooming brought me down to earth: taking him to the vet and being told I had to pull the hair out of his ears regularly and squirt hydrogen peroxide in them to clean out the wax made me question what I'd gotten myself into. (The vet's bill was a clue.) Peppi had to be brushed daily with a slicker and groomed every six weeks or his hair would become matted into curls like a Rastafarian's dreadlocks. And you know how people distrust those locks, sniffing the air for marijuana. I had to brush Peppi's teeth no less. Then I was instructed on nail clipping. Since I bite my own nails and have never had a manicure, I began to feel this dog would get more personal care from me than I gave myself. I only get a haircut every six months, and my cut was cheaper. Still, I was beginning to get used to the idea he'd be around for a while.

I found myself getting more and more into his world. "Isn't that your favorite hydrant?" I asked the day when he didn't stop to leave his mark where all the neighborhood dogs had announced their own visits. At first turned off by this behavior, I began to see that in dog culture, it's a kind of ephemeral graffiti, like "Peppi was here." When he took to only pooping on a mound of ice or snow, I attributed it to some discriminating dog judgment.

But I sometimes got irritated and critical. (Was the honeymoon truly over?) While walking at a fast clip several blocks to the park, I found myself not smelling the daisies or gazing raptly at the western horizon as it revealed itself between the trees around Cheesman Park. Instead, I stared at my little dog's rear legs. Never, I observed, does he approach our walks visually. Eyes ahead like a soldier, he's always got his nose to the ground. And my eyes are on the ground, too, since one of his favorite street foods is cat droppings, the eating of which greatly offends me. It has no nutritional value.

We used to love the same things, but then he strayed. At first when we were in our neighborhood park, I would let him off the leash thinking he'd romp and play like he did with me in the backyard, but instead he would head for the road and cause a traffic jam or collision. So I kept him on the leash, and then his favorite thing was to tow me along from one doggy jogger plop of poop to the next, as though we were at an Easter-egg hunt. Part of the hunt ritual was finding a good smell, like a dead animal scent, and rolling around in it until his furcoat was so "shtinky." I would invite him to take it off before he came into the apartment to permeate our den with its scent.

Our big breakthrough came after much mutual patience and obedience school. When we had three classes under his leash, we no longer went for a "drag." He finally walked around like a good little pooch, and I rewarded him by letting him loose in the apartment building. Peppi had been engaging in a strong flirtation with the curly white Bichon Frise upstairs, whom he didn't have to leave home to run into. He just sneaked out the door when I opened it to get the mail and bounded up the stairs, dog tags clinking. Soon I would hear double clinking and bounding, and a little white fluff ball named Popcorn bounced into the air in response to Peppi's invitation to play a game of tag. These are my fondest memories.

I no longer take early morning and nightly walks. I don't stand in doorways and talk to perfect strangers about "bitches." I don't chase after Peppi when he does not obey the "stay" command. "Stay" was the last command Peppi learned in obedience school. At the end of that week, on a full-moon night, Peppi woke me at 3 a.m. to pee, and we went into the backyard. It was dark, the fence gate was open, and Peppi got away. I never got to say "stay." All I can think is that he had a helluva last night. He must have caroused for hours. He never came to my calls, but at 9 a.m. the next morning I got a phone call that he had been killed by a car; it had happened at 7 a.m.

Guilt-ridden and grief stricken, I was advised by a stranger about the laws of love. Once you have loved and lost one animal, she said, you have more to give the next. I practiced this thinking and, two months later, got my present poodle, Comet, who has far more privileges than I allowed Peppi, and who receives the best I have to give, knowing what it can feel like to lose my best friend.

I take comfort in knowing that Peppi had a hambone that last night, and for the first time in the two months we'd been together, he had succumbed with pleasure to a brushing earlier in the evening. I knew he had always wanted to nose around the dumpsters in the alleys behind

York Street, and he must have done that to his heart's content.

There's only one heart broken between us now. Thanks, Peppi. You paved the way for me to have and love a pet. I will have more love for the next one just having known you.

Comet, the Maurice Chevalier of poodles.

Pig Tales

(1997 Howlings)

When Carol, my landlady, brought home her new Vietnamese pot-bellied pig, Louise was a cute little piglet, a football-on-spikes with a schnozzle. She made soft little oinks and kissed her owner whenever Carol balanced a piggy biscuit on her lips.

I didn't think Louise was cute for long. Her character flaw lay in the combination of her intelligence, persistence and relentless pursuit of the eternal food morsel from every last corner of her world: every last thread on the rug, crack in the floor, blade of grass on the lawn, piece of paper from the trash, and every nook and cranny in the blankets and couches. She was a munching, gnashing, snarfing, gobbling and swilling machine.

To encourage Louise to do her personal business in the backyard, Carol put in a series of doggie doors. I didn't have a dog door, so I used to leave my door cracked for my canine companion, Comet, to access the yard.

On a regular basis, as a side trip to the backyard, Louise would nose her way into my apartment and noisily snarf up Comet's food from his dish, making these gnashing "nerf-nerf" sounds that sent my blood pressure rocketing. I'd be in my waterbed, reading or grading papers or just relaxing, and in would come Louise. I'd hear that grunting "nerf-nerf" and scream, "Louise! Get out of here!" and she wouldn't even budge her nose from the bowl until she saw me through her peripheral vision come barreling around the

2002. Amused by my story of Louise, Irene Dogmatic, pet portrait painter, drew this illustration.

corner. She was so fast, like the metaphorical greased lightening. I, on the other hand, rising from a waterbed, then needing to grab my crutches, was never fast enough to catch her.

I told Carol, "I don't mind Popcorn (her little white dog) coming over here and eating, but Louise...I don't know, Carol, it really bothers me."

"But I don't understand why you mind Louise when you let Popcorn do it." To Carol, these were equally adorable pets.

"Because she's a PIG!" I sputtered. "She's...she's ...she's invasive...she snorts while she eats. She eats like it's her last meal on earth. Like she hasn't eaten in weeks, for God's sake! It's not even eating, it's inhaling and snorting the food at the same time. I can't explain it." I was beside myself with hostility. This hurt Carol, so of course, I didn't continue with my thought: "I don't like her because she reminds me of everything I hate in myself and all humans when they act PIGGY!!"

The first angry episode happened in the back hall, where I found Louise had gnawed her way through the huge, thick paper sack of dog food I kept stashed there. Gobbling as fast and as much as she could with every inhalation, nerf-nerfing like a jackhammer vacuum cleaner at high speed, spit slobbering all around her snout, frantically finishing up before I could reach her, Louise triggered my rage at every element in my existence over which I had no control. Stealing from the dog's dish was bad enough, but in this pig-out she consumed twenty times as much food. I screamed at her at twenty times my usual amplitude. LOUISE! WAIT 'TIL I CATCH YOU!! I'M GONNA KILL YOU!

Part of my consternation was that I was always one step behind her. After that incident, I put the dog food on a high stool where I figured she couldn't reach it. She knocked the stool over. I came home to Louise devouring my dog's food once again at her high-gnashing velocity. She was so smart that she also figured out how to get into the rabbit food that Carol had stored in special bins in the hallway. Soon, every one of Carol's storage bins had to be placed elsewhere. Louise was so clever she even figured out how to break into the rabbit's cage and steal the rabbit's food from its hutch in the backyard. (We had wondered who was letting the rabbit out when night after night a neighbor had found and returned him. Who would have thought?) After that, Carol had the rabbit door spring-loaded.

It was in the middle of the winter when Louise and I collided. Because our apartment building's back door locks automatically, I propped open the door as I left in my shirtsleeves to take out the trash. Louise bolted inside through the dog door, dislodging the prop and locking me outside in the process. I was livid! Then I remembered. My apartment door was open! Louise could get in! I walked around the building freezing and fuming, no one home in the building. I finally decided to mount the rabbit house and climb through my bedroom window. Balancing on top of a four-foot-high rabbit hut, throwing my crutches through the window, setting aside things that could break if they fell off the bureau, I hoisted myself in.

The first thing to greet me was the overturned trash bag under my window, where Louise had routed around and found some orange peels and a pizza box to chomp on. I bolted into the living room, where she'd eaten the tops of the fresh carnations and was now beyond in my work room with her head in the overturned trashcan.

My heart began to beat wildly. I ran back to the kitchen and shut the door and then back to the living room where I locked the entry like a thief. I had her cornered. I then proceeded to chase Louise from one end of my apartment to the other for at least ten manic minutes. Running as fast as I could on one leg, thrashing at her thick pigskin flanks with my crutches — one crutch to walk, one to whack — I could barely catch up to her.

Hauling her huge, fat, sausage body on four dainty legs, her pointy little hooves slipping and sliding and tapping across the hardwood floors faster than the scurry of a rat, she screeched indescribably, oinking out of this deep, hollow, protesting, bestial space inside her two-foot frame. When she reached one end of the apartment, she'd skid to a corner, and I'd get in a few good whacks for several seconds while she reversed direction, and then she'd run for it again with a swiftness denied by her body image but proved by her legs. Try as I might, I never once smacked her on her snout, which, I learned, is where pigs really do feel pain. Mostly I just scared the jeebers out of her, satisfying my hunger for revenge by extracting those blood-curdling cries of protest.

Finally the thought that Carol might come home and hear me, and then the thought that I might be perceived as torturing someone's poor innocent pet, caused me to slacken my pace. My rabid response to Louise's invasion of my apartment curtailed, I quite civilly invited her out the front door, thinking to myself: At least I won't see her around here for a while.

It took only 15 minutes. I was in my waterbed, and she was back at the dog dish. Soon after that I let Carol know I had reached my limits with Louise.

In response, Carol's dad put up a divider between my apartment and the back hall so Comet could jump over it to exit, but Louise couldn't come in. Carol put my dog food in a huge utility trashcan with a lid like a tamper-proof prescription bottle. Pig-proof, I was assured.

Louise worked at it every day, and finally, when the dog food supply got down to one-fourth of its 50-pound size, Louise was able to overturn the barrel. With her industrial proboscis, she literally nosed her way through the clamp on the lid, and when I came out to empty the trash, I found her with her head in the barrel grunting away in ecstasy.

"You filthy, stinking PIG!! I'M GONNA GET YOU!" I felt another encounter coming on. With primal urgency, however, she stepped through her dog door, briskly waddling her rear end and beating her long skinny tail in happiness and victory.

Carol's partner, Karen, who owned half the building and had no allegiance to the pig, caught me in this rage and, I suspect, was the origin of the phone call to the zoning and health departments.

First to arrive was the zoning administrator. "I've heard there's a mean pig in the building." Well, she did try to bite my cleaning lady's toes when Donna tried to shoo her away from the trash, but I couldn't bring myself to say she was mean. After all, it was her nature to protect her food, right? The health department officer who came to see me pulled out a pad of paper and started to take notes. "Have you seen the pig chase people through the hallways and try to bite them?" From Karen I heard that something like this had happened, but it hadn't happened to me.

In earnest and with emphasis I replied, "I don't know if she chased anyone," I paused and, knowing I might be inviting further questioning, went on anyway, "but I have certainly chased that pig!"

Age 13, in the front lawn, across the street from the library and the high school, on Beach Street, Revere. Confirmation day.

Calamity Jane
(1999 Have Crutch Will Travel, revised 2002)

"How are ya?" The doctor pulled up a chair next to my hospital bed, and, while holding the clipboard with one hand, he extended the other in greeting. He then proceeded through the long list of questions I had already answered six or seven times during the earlier hospital admissions process.

He wanted to know how I injured my back, came to have a scoliosis, how I had developed pressure sores which prevented me from sitting, and how I came to be on this unit. Of course, he had all the notes, but they each have to hear it for themselves. Some are nicer than others. He was a very polite and rather handsome man the same age as me, about 45.

"And how long have you had this phantom limb pain?"

"For 25 years. Ever since I lost my leg."

"So, you've dealt with chronic pain for 25 years. And I see from this note here that you're depressed. Have you been going through this depression for quite some time?"

I had to hold back from snorting at him, and I did say with some exasperation: "Are you kidding me?" I was tired of that diagnosis, that word. Who wouldn't be depressed in my situation? I had come to Denver to make my living and I was failing. I had cried my share of frustration's angry tears, but I was also capable of catharsis.

"'Depression' is my middle name," I told him.

I wasn't satisfied with that adjective. It sounded so … trite? … No. Unfinished. Untrue and I didn't want to be glib.

Before he could say anything else, I added: "And my last name is 'Get over it.'" There. I felt almost accounted for, but a nagging wish followed quickly on its heels. Oh, I wish this doctor would flirt with me, banter, have some fun, say what came to my mind as the natural conclusion of the repartee:

"And your first name is…?"

I imagined myself poised, upright. I'd sit, like a good little girl (the one I wasn't when my seventh grade home room teacher called me by that name first) and say sweetly,

"Calamity."

I'd say it coyly, with melody, and maybe he'd see the humor. However, that was unlikely. For the audience to get a joke based on an allusion, the joke has to pass through a shared memory bank. How would a doctor know the name I had been christened with because of my ready excuses for why I was late for home room, or what had happened to the homework I didn't turn in?

Mr. Hoover called me Calamity Jane all through the seventh grade. He'd heard enough stories over time about what happened to my homework to conclude that my personality was born of disaster. First he suspected me of being Pinocchio, but after grilling the class for both the contents and answers to the assignments, and I was always raising my hand, he concluded I was either a genius or had a good enough memory to get credit for the assignment even though I failed to produce the necessary documents.

I was very creative. Many excuses involved dogs, and/or one of my many family members.

"Uh, Ms. Kenney, where is your homework?"

"I did do it, but my mother used the paper by mistake to light the stove." The utilities company turned off the gas at our home when my mother couldn't pay the bill, and so we really did use the coal stove for heat. The other kids always laughed at me when I reported these things, and maybe they didn't believe me, but for some strange reason, although I was embarrassed of my home, I was not embarrassed by this routine storytelling. (Hadn't my mother always said I was a "brazen" child?)

Another time I said, "I did do it, but my sister crumbled it up while I was working." I'd thought that that story would do, but he was waiting for more.

"I accept crumbled homework, Ms. Kenney."

Uh oh. Gotta improvise." ... so I hit her, and then my father punished me by tearing it up." I always had my father be the bad parent. He was, so that felt fair enough.

"Well, next time bring the scraps in," Mr. Hoover scowled.

The next time, though, my homework flew out the window of the bus, and I had to explain: The scraps were blowin' in the wind!

Could that have really happened? I think it did. I know one time George Grasso did hold my notebook out the window of the bus and threaten to let it go. It's hard now to remember which stories were true, which stories of my chaotic family life were genuine and which were fictions. However, the time the dog ate my science experiment was a true event. A real calamity.

The science experiment called for us to cut up a potato into slices and weigh them — first fresh, and then when they were old. I think the point was to notice that they did lose weight, and that weight was glucose - or was it water? Anyway, it was supposed to make a strong impression about dehydration. The scale used to perform this experiment was fashioned from two different cut-off lunch milk cartons held up by strings, balanced by some contraption easily found in grade school environments. We measured the differential of the potato specimens with weights carefully made of folded-up one-inch squares of tinfoil.

When I showed up for science class without my homework, I had to account for not only the measuring scale, but all those bits of aluminum and a cut-up potato.

"I was taking a short cut to school because I missed the bus, and a big dog chased me through the woods. A black one. He caught up to me and I tripped, and he ate the potatoes."

The science teacher's arms crossed his chest. Oh, how difficult to convey to him the terror of that occasion, an animal chasing after me, and now a whole science experiment and the results! Gone! How little pleasure I was getting this time from the class's laughter as I gave my accounting. This time I am telling the truth! I did do my science experiment. And they're still laughing. I began to doubt myself. Why did these upsets always seem to happen to me? Why was the truth so hard to believe? Was Calamity Jane always in trouble like me because there was something wrong with her? Did she feel the same shame?

Calamity Jane must have always been late for school, I concluded, and she probably did a lot of praying when she was a little kid, because when you're a real little kid, you can't always run fast enough to make it to school on time.

Seeking sanctuary in the hospital as an adult, a single, disabled woman coming to the end of her abilities, resources and wits, and with no one to turn to, I felt a little like that now with this good-looking doctor. "It's not my fault," I wanted to say. I wanted to say what I felt like saying to Mr. Hoover in seventh grade, but I waited for the doctor to finish his intake.

"It says here you have been suffering from "adjustment disorder." Do you know what you are having a hard time adjusting to?"

Where do they get these diagnoses? I looked him straight in the eyes, and I said, "Life without a Visa card."

There. Finally I knew what was wrong with me. They named it; "a disorder." No one even had to tell me what I was not adjusting to. When I first saw I was going to have to go into debt, I considered it spiritual failure. (The alternative was worse; I was clear suicide was the least moral of the options.) Who could adjust to being in too much pain to work, but doing it anyway, making the pain worse, and having to live on both $500/month and a part time teacher's salary that paid just enough to cover my dentist bill for the year?

I knew not to tell him too much, because nowadays "everybody's a victim," according to the socio-economic-psycho-logicians, and I know from experience there's nothing like having the victim bear the brunt of responsibility, especially the ones who looked too good to be true.

Me, I was more inclined to blame the system. The whole thing with the government program I was part of, something called PASS [Plan for Achieving Self-Support], had been temporarily "suspended." They call it a "moratorium" when the US General Accounting Office under the new republican congress was looking for ways to slash budget figures and create a tax return. The PASS program had been going on 20 years, and in 1995, the suspension hit many disabled people, poised for success, like a foot to the throat. Homes, businesses, health, even lives of precious human beings were threatened and lost, but ... once again, that's another story, one of the best ones I know because of the activist disabled people who led the PASS Participants Rights Campaign in Denver and across the country.

I dared not say anything bad about Social Security because you have to be grateful you aren't selling pencils in the subway. However, I loved to think of it as unsocial insecurity, as one of my disabled friends once added the prefixes on the wall of a social security office we had occupied and thus brought the federal police down on our protest.

So, to this concerned physician, I just mentioned I had bailed myself out of a health and household security problem by using my Visa.

I could see I had gotten to him. He smiled ever so slightly. Engaged. He didn't write anything down, he just said: "You lost your credit? How?"

I nodded. Rather than go into the infinitely painful details of losing the life raft I'd been floating on for the past five years as I lived beyond my means, which were pitifully minimal, I nodded and counted on imagination and compassion from him.

"I lost my quality of life. I may not be able to keep my car, or my health club for swimming, or treat my scoliosis pain with massage from here on. I will lose my business. I will be adjusting for a long time."

"What happened to your credit?" He was genuinely interested.

So I told him this much. I'd been paying for medical bills and subsidizing my Social Security Disability Income with my credit card, giving me enough to have a car and keep an office running. Once I reached my max, there was no more money for medication.

I was in so much pain the depression and the pain became one and the same. My intestines reacted with a three-month long case of diarrhea. I was cleaning it off the walls. When there was no way out for me, I just called my doctor, and said I cannot take it anymore. That implies suicidal ideation. I voluntarily booked myself into the hospital so I would not get any more hurt than I already was.

But, I pointed out to him; I met the deadline of the most recent issue of the magazine I published, by bringing my laptop into the hospital, finishing the layout, and having my network of friends shuttle the file to the printer and then the magazine to the bookstores.

"Why did you let it get this bad?" he said, obviously missing my point about how the deck was stacked — because you are supposed to just survive, not thrive, in the system.

Here I was in a psych ward hoping someone would see me for something besides a calamity. Will some things ever change?

The answer is yes. They did change. In miraculous ways that involved total strangers, second chances, a new friend, and progress. I got a medication that quieted my riotous pain, I paid off all my debt, established new credit; when I couldn't work anymore, I was given money to live on. A benefit was held; friends and strangers and angels appeared. I became eligible for a loan for home ownership. I would buy a home that could adjust to me and my disability, instead of the reverse. I would make order out of the disorder. I would make Calamity Jane proud.

A friend sent me a copy of a little book, *The Adventures of Calamity Jane*, "by Herself," as the author Marthy Jane Cannery put it. What a life she had! She lived out on the frontier and took risks most women wouldn't dare. She was a champion rider and shooter. She had plenty of close calls, but most importantly, she lived to talk about them. And she wrote her stories down. She was a heroine and a storyteller. She wasn't a calamity; she just wrote about them.

I can finally accept Calamity Jane as a nickname.

But Mr. Hoover, just so you know, all the stories in this book are true.

1997, Winter Park, showing off for an Associated Press story by reporter Helen O'Neil. Photo by Byron Hoetzl.

We appreciate and prefer electronic orders of *Have Crutch Will Travel*. To order go to www.howlings.com. We will fulfill your order as soon as we receive your payment in the mail. However, if you do not have e-mail, please send this order form with your check or money order for $20.00 U.S. ($35.00 CAN) plus $5 shipping and handling, per copy:

Name_____

Address _____

_____

City_____

State or Province _____

Zip or Postal Code_____

Area Code _____ Telephone # _____

Email _____

Quantity (number of books)   _____
      X $20.00=   _____
Plus shipping & handling $5 =   _____
     (Total amount due)   _____

Mail to: Tell Tale Publishing
          Box 181172
          Denver, CO 80218

Please allow 4 to 6 weeks for delivery

Inquire at:
http://www.howlings.com

Thank you for your order.

Sorry, no CODs